PARENTING

Successful Church Leaders Share Biblical Principles for Raising Kids in the Nineties

Compiled and Edited by
Hal Donaldson
Kenneth M. Dobson

Parenting
Compiled and Edited by
Hal Donaldson and Kenneth M. Dobson

Printed in the United States of America
ISBN: 1-880689-02-2
Copyright 1993, Onward Books, Inc.

Cover design by Matt Key

The opinions contained herein do not necessarily represent the views of other participants.

Unless otherwise noted, Scripture quotations are taken from the *New International Version.* Copyright 1973, 1978, 1984, International Bible Society. Scripture quotations marked *NKJV* are taken from the *New King James Version.* Copyright 1979, 1980, 1982, Thomas Nelson, Inc., Publishers. Scripture quotations marked *KJV* are from the *King James Version* of the Bible. Scripture quotations marked *TLB* are taken from *The Living Bible,* copyright 1971 by Tyndale House Publishers, Wheaton, Illinois. Scripture quotations marked *NASB* are taken from the *New American Standard Bible,* copyright 1960, 1962, 1963, 1968, 1971, 1972, 1975, 1977, The Lockman Foundation.

All rights reserved. No portion of this book may used without written permission of the publisher, with the exception of brief excerpts for magazine articles, reviews, etc. For further information or permission, write Onward Books, P. O. Box 292305, Sacramento, CA 95829.

Contents

The Family Unit

1. For Men Only 11
   Dave Roever
2. Building a Healthy Home 25
   Paul Goulet
3. Family Fundamentals 33
   Sammy Vazquez
4. Better Family Communication 43
   Norm Schulz
5. The Single Parent 53
   Scott Hagan

Relationships

6. Peer Pressure: The Unfriendly Fire 65
   Donnie Moore
7. Choosing a Mate 75
   Paul Olson
8. Searching for Heroes 83
   Scott Gossenberger
9. Resolving Conflict 99
   Kelly S. Goins
10. The Bible, Respect, and Authority 109
    Walt Weaver

Behavior

11. The Power Generation 119
    Rob Hoskins
12. Sex and Dating 133
    Steve Wilson
13. Understanding Teenagers 155
    Donny Burleson
14. Clothes, Hair, and Makeup 165
    Randy Greer
15. Movies, Music, and More 179
    Lynn Wheeler

Spiritual Life

16. God, Kids, and Youth Ministry 195
    Michael De Vito
17. Keeping Kids in Church 203
    Glenn R. Embree
18. The Love Factor 215
    Coco Perez
19. Kids 'In Christ' 225
    Kevin Newton
20. God in the Public School 237
    James 'Rat' Saunders

Character Development

21. The Power of Encouragement 247
    Billy Williams
22. Developing Discipline in Kids 261
    Steve Thomas
23. Whatever Happened to Values? 277
    Barry Sappington
24. The Family Game Plan 291
    Larry Rust

Endnotes 299

Foreword

The statistics are staggering, the stories heartwrenching. It is obvious to anyone who watches Dan Rather's "Eye on America" or reads the polls in *USA Today:* America's youth are in crisis.

Millions of young people are searching for answers, meaning and hope. One only needs to peer into their uncertain eyes and study their stern facades and guarded smiles to know their "quiet desperation."

The pressures and temptations facing young people today are mounting: drugs, alcohol, sex, crime and more. Tragically, America's children are not being taught the moral principles necessary to cope with these pressures, nor is the family unit strong enough to help them evade life's temptations. Many children, after all, are on their own. Their parents are too preoccupied with their own survival and quest for happiness to worry about nurturing a young life.

Because the challenges facing America's youth are mounting, the job of parenting is increasingly difficult. Thus, it is imperative that parents understand the biblical blueprint for raising God-fearing children. *Parenting* is a collection of ideas and principles from Scripture, which will help you guide your children as they endeavor to make quality decisions and maneuver through life unscathed.

Raising children can be an imposing, frustrating challenge at times. Nonetheless, kids are one of God's greatest gifts—priceless lives entrusted to parents by a heavenly Father. And because God loves children, He desires to give parents insight into shaping and nurturing their offspring. He wants children to serve Him. He wants them to achieve their potential. He wants them to make their parents proud.

There is little doubt that *Parenting* is one of those tools God has birthed in the hearts of its editors and authors to help you and your children. One only has to look at the list of contributing authors to know this is a quality effort. It features men like Dave Roever and Donnie Moore who have spent years helping parents, teens and children.

I trust this book will encourage you to invest wisely in your children, to "train them in the way they should go." Their future, to a large extent, will be determined by what you give them today.

Rich Wilkerson

Acknowledgments

Special thanks to Sharon Sousa for her assistance in editing. Heartfelt appreciation to Deb Petrosky, Matt Key, Randy Cole, Steve Wilson, David Donaldson, Rob Clay, and Billy Williams.

THE FAMILY UNIT

*The life of the state rests and must ever rest
upon the life of the family . . .*

Theodore Roosevelt

1

For Men Only

DAVE ROEVER

As I tour the country's high schools sharing my story of tragedy-turned-triumph, I take time at the end of a presentation to visit with the kids one-on-one. I probe their minds trying to get a handle on what's causing this generation to wallow in a quagmire of hopelessness, despair, and turmoil. Whatever the topic of conversation, I ultimately come back to two basic questions: What about your home? What about your dad?

In answer to the first question, I occasionally hear, "Great . . . my parents are great." But to the second, all too often, the response is: "My dad left when I was little," or "My dad's hardly ever home," or "My dad lives outside the state, so I don't see him or talk to him much."

Another thing I've noticed as I tour the country is that our church congregations are made up of older people. Where are the children? The teenagers?

This isn't going to be another church-bashing session. I'm not blaming the church. In the past few years we've had all the church-bashing we can take; I'm not going to add to it. The difficulties we face in America today are not the fault of the church.

BETRAYED AND VIOLATED

After finishing a high school assembly in the northern United States, I opened the floor for questions and comments. A young lady stood in front of her 2,500 peers and said, "Mr. Roever, every night my father comes into my room and tries to sexually molest me. I have to run out of the house to get away from him." She hesitated a second, then in measured, calculated words, asked, "Mr. Roever, how can I get rid of my father?"

The most common statement made to me by girls in public schools is, "Mr. Roever, I wish you were my dad." My son and daughter are young adults now, but if either of them ever said to another man, *I wish you were my dad*, it would break my heart. Yet, I hear it every day, over and over again.

During an assembly in Michigan a few weeks later, I told the story of the girl who'd asked how to get rid of her father. When I finished my presentation, the kids lined up all the way to the back of the gym, waiting to speak to me. Most of them just wanted a hug—just wanted to hear somebody say *I love you*. At least a dozen times while doing an assembly, I tell the kids I love them, but that's not enough. They want me to look them in the eye and say it just to them.

This particular day, a little seventeen-year-old blonde sitting on the front row waited until everyone finished before she stepped up to me, grabbed my arm, and pulled me aside. "Mr. Roever, my name is Sasha," she said. Her eyes revealed a frantic young woman. When she spoke again, her words were barely audible, but desperate. "Please, Mr. Roever, what did you tell that girl?"

Taking Sasha's hand, I asked, "Do you have a problem at home?"

She nodded as tears filled her eyes. I knew if I asked her another question I would be involved, because if she answered it with a yes—and there wasn't the slightest doubt in my mind she would—I would break the law if I didn't report it. I plunged in. "Are you being sexually abused by your father?"

"Yes," she said, embarrassed and ashamed.

The details that followed defy comprehension by decent human beings. She said, "I was almost three years old when my dad left us. He was gone for nearly ten years. When my mom begged him to come back, he said he would . . . on one condition . . . I wouldn't be a virgin when I turned thirteen." Sasha struggled to empty her soul of the awful story. "My mother said yes . . . and . . . and I've had to sleep with my dad for four years . . . and I hate it . . . and I want out."

I called Danny, the youth pastor who had driven me to Sasha's school that day. "Danny," I said, "I need two counselors. I want Christian counselors, but they have to be state-approved. I need help and I need it now. Is there anyone you know?"

His eyes grew wide as he said, "You're not going to believe what happened! Early this morning I got a phone call from a couple in our church who work for the State of Michigan as counselors! They said, 'We want to see Dave Roever in action in a public school. Can you get us into the assembly?' I called the school and got permission for them to come. They're waiting in the foyer right now."

Sasha never spent another night with her father. The counselors placed her with a good family, and that evening in our crusade she gave her heart to Jesus. Sasha faithfully attends church and is growing in the Lord, no longer tormented by fear of what her father might do next.

This story has a tragic twist to it. When Danny, his pastor and wife, and the counselors took Sasha to tell her parents what the state was doing and how the church was cooperating, they discovered the parents attended church regularly. After getting Sasha settled in her new home, Danny spoke with the parents' pastor. His comment? "You take Sasha for now. When you get her straightened out, bring her back to me and we'll take it from there."

Sasha found two more girls in her school who were in abusive situations. One had been abused by her father, the other by her high school coach. These men are sitting behind bars today and, as far as I'm concerned, they can throw away the keys.

EPIDEMIC PROPORTIONS

Statistics indicate that twenty-five to forty percent of American women today have been sexually abused by a family member. And it doesn't occur only in families outside the church. All around us are individuals who have experienced sexual abuse. Many of them are angry and bitter and harbor a burning desire for revenge. Often the offender is dead and gone, but the wounds of the victims are still painful.

Many young people in America are living in hell on earth with no end in sight. The fastest growing cause of death among teens—next to drinking and driving—is suicide. Consumed with despair, they feel they have nothing to live for and suicide is their only way out. These are the kids I face regularly in the schools of our nation.

God save our children. Our greatest natural resource, if you can call it that, is our kids. It's not oil; it's not technology; it's our children. And what's being done to many of them is incomprehensible.

A CHALLENGE FOR FATHERS

By now, you've probably figured out where I'm heading. This is a gut-wrenching subject, and one that's difficult to discuss, but I challenge you to keep reading. The problem in America is not the government; it's not the schools; it's not the church. The problem is Dad. So when we're through blaming the government, the schools, and the church, we finally have to admit the responsibility lies with us.

Some of the last words of the Old Testament say it clearly: "Behold, I will send you Elijah the prophet before the coming of the great and dreadful day of the Lord. And He will turn the hearts of the fathers to the children" (Malachi 4:5,6, NKJV). That means fathers' hearts have not been where they should be. And now, just before it's too late, just in the nick of time, the heart of the father must be turned to his children, and the hearts of the children to the father. Why? "Lest I come and strike the earth with a curse" (Malachi 4:6, NKJV). I hate threats, but I love a challenge. Challenge me and I'll go the last mile; I'll go miles past the last mile; I'll overrun the objective in my eagerness to accept a challenge because I believe in challenges. *Lest I come and strike the earth with a curse* can be taken as a threat or challenge. If it's a threat, it may be too late. If it's a challenge, we have an opportunity to prevent it from coming to pass. I prefer to take that verse as a challenge.

PRIEST AND PROVIDER

Every husband/father is called to be the priest and provider of his home. If you think you're a good provider, but you're a lousy priest, you're kidding yourself. There's no such thing as a good provider who is not a good priest. Nor is there a good priest who is not a good provider. A good priest will always provide for his family; that's an automatic. But I caution you, Dad, if you give your kids Izod shirts and Air-Jordan shoes every day of their lives but don't have the love of God in your home, you're a lousy provider.

You may say, "I'm a good priest, Dave. I pray for my family." When was the last time your kids heard you call their names before the throne of God? It's not too late to start. Pray for your children. Intercede for them. Let them hear you. If they can't hear you when you pray, then pray by the air-conditioning vent. Pray for the sins they thought you didn't know about, and let them experience a few sleepless nights wondering how in the world you found out. All over America I deal with kids whose lives are shattered. I'm convinced it wouldn't be so if they regularly heard their fathers pray.

Mothers, I'm not ignoring you. I know many of you have carried the load and been the priestesses of your households because your husbands have ignored their God-given responsibility. Thank you for being godly women, but it's time for men to assume spiritual leadership of their homes.

SHOW AND TELL

Many fathers have never said the words "I love you" to their children. You may be one of them. You think they *know* you love them, but if you don't tell them they can't be sure. Tell your kids you love them, then show it by sharing your life with them. Dad, turn your heart to your children. Don't let anything take precedence over them. If your company offers you a ten-times-your-regular-pay raise to do a job that would send you to Timbuktu when your little girl is being smooth-talked by some boy in school and she's about to give away her virginity because she thinks she's giving him her love, don't take the job! Stay with your daughter. I'd lose my job, pick up aluminum cans, and sell them to feed my family—for the rest of my life if necessary—before I'd put my daughter on the altar of sacrifice for my personal success.

Lose your job, but don't lose your children.

Take your boy fishing and hunting. I'd rather go hunting *with* my son today than go hunting *for* him tomorrow.

HEROES

I'm tired of seeing our children turn to the rock-and-roll gods of this generation in search of heroes. They have posters all over their walls, and they bow down before their gods at rock concerts. They ought to have better role models than rock stars who do drugs then say, "Don't do drugs." The kids see through it; they know most of the rock stars are just trying to appease irate parents. So, in essence, they're setting two examples for today's youth: one of lying, the other of drug abuse.

I think Dad ought to be the hero in the family. What's this nonsense of turning silly little *teenage neutered midget turtles* into heroes? I thank God my kids had more to look up to than neutered turtles living in a sewer! There's got to be more for our children. Give them a dad to look up to, and when someone asks who their hero is, they'll say, "Dad's my hero."

How do you become a hero? Be a man of your word. When you make a promise, live by it. If you break a promise, go to your children and explain why you can't do what you said you'd do. And make sure your reason for not doing what you promised is more important than doing it. The integrity of a father's word is a standard for the lives of his children. Unfortunately, for many of America's kids today, no standard exists. There's no dad to be a hero.

Believe it or not, you can be a hero by saying no. Your kids may be saying, "Aw, Dad!" on the outside, but inside they're saying, *Thank you! You gave me a reason to say no when I didn't have the courage to say it on my own.*

Another way to be a hero to your kids is to treat their mother with love and respect. Call her *honey,* not *heifer.* Tell her you love her everyday—right in front of the kids. Tell her three, four, five times a day. They need to hear you say it. Send your wife flowers; not just for her but for your kids as well. When they come home from school and see them, they'll say, "Oooo, Mom, where did the flowers come from?" The look on her face when she says, "Your dad sent them" will speak volumes to your kids. They find great security in knowing that Mom and Dad love each other.

Be a gentleman. It may seem old-fashioned to open a door for your wife, or help her on with her coat, but some things never go out of style. Besides that, it's scriptural. Ephesians 5:25 says to love your wife like Jesus loves the church and treat your wife like Jesus treats the church. He gives the church gifts; He opens the door; He shows His goodness and kindness, and He says "I love you." We ought to do the same. Don't be so busy you don't have time for a little kindness along the way.

I may not be the best at chivalry, but I had the best teacher a man could want. My daddy treated my mama with respect. He walked into the kitchen every morning, bent down and kissed the back of her neck right in front of us kids, and said, "Lois, darling, I love you." We thought it was funny and we'd snicker and say, "Daddy's kissing Mama!" But he taught me how to treat my wife by the example he set.

Not long ago Dad stepped into a room in his three-piece suit and walked up to Mama's casket. He bent down, brushed the hair from her ear and said, "Lois, darling, I love you." My dad kept his vows unto death. That's why he's my hero.

A friend named Lee Williams lost his wife and two daughters when a drunk driver sped down the wrong side of an interstate highway and killed twenty-seven passengers on a church bus.[1] Lee's wife and two daughters were his entire family. Two years after the tragedy, I asked Lee how he was doing.

"Pretty good, Dave. . . . I just came from the cemetery. I don't get there often, but I had a promise to keep. Kristen would have been sixteen this week, and I promised her sixteen roses on her sixteenth birthday, so I made a trip up to Missouri and put them on her grave. You know, Dave, a dad's got to keep his word." He continued, "Robin's grave is right beside Kristen's. The color of her phone is kinda faded now. . . . I promised her a phone of her own on her fourteenth birthday. A man has to keep his promises."

You say, "Dave, the kids are dead. You don't keep vows to dead people." You're right. Lee was keeping vows to *himself*.

Dad, if you're going to turn your heart to your children, you have a few promises to keep—to yourself and to them.

There are things you said you would do that you haven't done. It's time to do them. For your kids' sake, give them a hero.

RESPONSIBILITY: A TWO-WAY STREET

Every kid living at home has a responsibility, too. Not only does that verse say the fathers should turn their hearts to their children, but the children should turn their hearts to their fathers. Kids may ask, "How can I turn my heart to my father?" Start by telling him you love him. "But I don't love him. In fact, I think I hate him," you may say. Tell him you love him anyway. You may be as surprised as he is to find out you really do.

Keep *your* promises to your parents. Do your homework. Clean your room. Honor your father and mother. You have an obligation and a responsibility before God to do so. If you call yourself a Christian, you should behave as a child of God. If you don't, you're in double jeopardy.

Every child should make this pledge: "I solemnly vow I will clean my room. I will obey my father and mother. I will do my homework. I will be a child of God who accepts responsibility. And I will serve You, Lord Jesus, so help me God."

THE AWFUL TRUTH

When I spoke at a prayer breakfast in Alaska, the governor handed me a paper. The message on it has changed my life. It said:

Today in America . . .
2,795 teenagers will get pregnant
1,106 teenagers will have abortions

372 teenagers will have miscarriages
1,027 babies will be born to mothers addicted to cocaine
67 babies will die before they are 30 days old
105 babies will die before they are a year old
211 children will be arrested for drug abuse
437 children will be arrested for drinking and driving
10 children will die from gunshot wounds
30 children will be wounded by gunfire
135,000 children will take guns to school
1,512 teenagers will drop out of school
1,849 children will be abused or neglected
6 teenagers will commit suicide
3,288 children will run away from home
1,629 children are in adult jails
7,742 teens will become sexually active
623 teenagers will contract gonorrhea or syphilis[2]

Tomorrow in America it all starts all over again . . .

Dad, turn your heart to your children. Turn your heart to God. Don't be so proud or so arrogant as to think you're too big for correction. Don't be so senseless as to think you're too big to respond to the tug in your spirit. For the sake of your children, for your own sake, Dad, turn your heart to your kids.

When you stand before God on Judgment Day, the only thing you can take with you is your wife and children. You can't take your job. You can't take that gold watch signifying forty years of service. You can't take any of the things you thought were so important. The only thing you can take is your family. That's it. You can have all the gold watches that were ever made, but I'm sure you'd trade them in a New York second for the daughter who won't make it to heaven because you were too busy earning watches.

Dad, God loves you and so do I. I want God to do a miracle in your life today. Follow me in this simple prayer. Pray it only if you mean it. Let it come from your heart. This is an act of the priest; the responsibility of the priest; the duty, the performance—not the put-on. Speak it out like the man you are. I want God to hear you, and I want the devil to hear you, too:

> Lord Jesus, thank You. Thank You for Your love, Your patience, Your life, Your death, and Your resurrection. You are my High Priest; You intercede for me; You shed Your blood for me because You loved me. God, in those areas where I'm wrong—and You know them as well as I—please forgive me. Cleanse me of all filthiness of the flesh, mind, and spirit as I commit myself to You. As I study Your Word, I pray Your characteristics will become mine. Jesus, help me to be a man of my word. Help me to stand for what is right regardless of what the rest of the world may do. Give me the strength of the Holy Spirit to be the witness a dad ought to be. Thank You for my children. Thank You for my wife. Make me a holy priest, a godly priest, a priest filled with integrity. And now, as priest of my household, I hold my family before You and I intercede for them. I will not let go of them. Dear God, save my family, cleanse them, preserve their souls, and let us all stand in an unbroken circle around the throne of God.
>
> Satan, you're a liar. You've lied to me for years, but Jesus has set me free. The blood of Jesus cleanses and keeps my family. Satan, you no longer have any part in my family. You are finished; you are history. Jesus is Lord of my family, and we will stand

before Him in peace and love. In the name of Jesus Christ, Amen.

The Reverend Dave Roever, horribly burned when a white-phosphorus grenade exploded inches from his face in Vietnam, inspires thousands across the nation with his enthusiasm for life. Credentialed with the Assemblies of God for thirty years, and speaking for public high schools, television, business conventions, crusades, and churches, he crisscrosses America bringing a message of hope.

Dave attended Southwestern Assemblies of God College and currently serves as president for the Roever Evangelistic Association, Inc. and the Roever Educational Assistance Program, Inc.

He and his wife Brenda are the parents of son Matthew and daughter Kimberly Roever Chapin.

2

Building a Healthy Home

Paul Goulet

Since the fall of Adam and Eve, God's plan for the family has been challenged on every front by godless philosophies until the very concept of "family" is no longer recognizable. External forces plague our nation's children with violence, secular humanism, New Age teaching in public schools . . . while internal forces add to the destruction. In his book, *The Power of Parents' Words,* Norman Wright describes several problems that threaten the family from within:

Verbal and Emotional Abuse. I've heard parents—Christian as well as non-Christian—call their children degrading names such as "stupid," "pig," "devil," and "idiot." James 3:6-12 speaks about the destruction that thoughtless and unkind words can cause. Many parents wouldn't consider themselves abusive because they don't inflict physical pain on their children, but verbal and emotional abuse can be just as harmful. If we withhold love, express conditional love, berate or neglect, our children will suffer just as surely as if they were beaten.

Perfectionism. We all set goals and standards we want our children to strive for, but when those goals and standards are unrealistic, we deprive our children of the benefit of achievement. If they never quite measure up in our eyes, they'll either experience ongoing failure or they'll give up.

Rigidity. Rigidity refers to how firmly a parent insists that his way be adopted. It leaves no room for individualism or creative thinking. It stifles healthy growth and sets the stage for rebellion.

Repression. Our children should be able to safely express their thoughts, opinions, and feelings with us, but honest communication is hindered when the above conditions exist in the home. If children are belittled or criticized for their ideas, they'll become hesitant to express them. If they are unable to measure up, they'll quit trying. If they are denied the freedom to think for themselves, they'll be easily led astray.[1]

LOT'S EXAMPLE

Lot and his family are an example of a dysfunctional family. In many ways, they lived in a society much like our own. It was plagued by the same moral confusion that we experience today. How did Lot deal with the challenge of raising a healthy family in an unhealthy environment? Was he successful? If not, why not?

Lot was a righteous man: ". . . he [God] rescued Lot, a righteous man, who was distressed by the filthy lives of lawless men (for that righteous man, living among them day after day, was tormented in his righteous soul by the lawless deeds he saw and heard)" (2 Peter 2:7,8). Lot was also hospitable. He invited two strangers into his home, cooked them a meal, and gave them lodging for a night. (See Genesis 19:1-3.) But Lot made a poor choice when he moved to Sodom. To begin with, he pitched his tent *outside* Sodom, but he eventually moved into the city and became a prominent citizen. (See Genesis 13:12; 19:1.) As a result, he lost his wife and raised daughters who embraced a worldly view of morality (see Genesis 19:26,31-38).

How did Lot wind up in such a wicked environment? Why would he expose his family—and particularly his daughters—to such sinfulness? The answers aren't clear, but the account of Lot reinforces the need to establish boundaries between us and the world. It also offers three important lessons:

Do not compromise your morals and values. It's vital for the spiritual well-being of our children that we don't compromise our beliefs. We must be morally and ethically upright because our children follow our example. Lot compromised his beliefs and it cost him a great deal.

Live and communicate a life-changing faith. Ephesians 6:4 says: "Fathers, do not exasperate your children; instead, bring them up in the training and instruction of the Lord." Lot's family did not experience a life-changing faith. While Lot's family members were accountable for their decision to resist God's standards, their father's poor example undoubtedly contributed to it.

Obey God's Word. We should not allow our actions to contradict our words. When we say we are Christians but do not follow God's commands, we send the message that obedience isn't important. When many of Jesus' followers turned from Him, He asked the twelve if they would also leave. Peter answered, "Lord, to whom shall we go? You have the words of eternal life" (John 6:68). Do we live as if we believe God's Word brings eternal life? If *we* don't, our children won't.

NOAH'S EXAMPLE

Noah also dwelt in a vile and wicked society; so wicked that God decided to destroy mankind. Only Noah and his family were found to be righteous, and consequently their lives were spared. While Lot's family mocked him when he warned them of impending doom, Noah's family believed and helped build the ark. Noah refused to compromise, even when it meant standing alone. He was undoubtedly mocked and ridiculed but was nevertheless "blameless among the people of his time . . ." (Genesis 6:9). His righteous life made a difference in his family, and his relationship with God was passed down from generation to generation. Is our relationship with God one that our children should emulate? If not, we would do well to heed the lessons taught by these two men of the Bible.

A COMPARISON

A study in contrast between Lot and Noah provides seven points to help build a healthy home in a sick world:

Lead the way. Don't wait for someone else to be the spiritual leader where your family is concerned; that should be your responsibility—and your privilege. Noah did all that God commanded, while Lot delayed and tried to negotiate with the angels God sent to deliver him from impending doom. What would have happened if Noah had been like Lot? What if he had said the following:

> God, do we really need such a *big* boat? And gopher wood, of all things. Why not plywood? It's easier to get and not nearly so expensive. And God, I was thinking . . . couldn't we have a sun roof? And another thing . . . about all those animals . . . is that really necessary?

Fortunately for all of us, that's not how it was. God said, "Build it." Noah said, "Okay." God said, "Get in." Noah did just that. Are we as obedient to God, or are we more like Lot? That's a very important question when we look at the fate of our families.

Be willing to sacrifice. Imagine devoting more than one hundred years to build a boat. Who paid for it? Where did the wood come from? Did Noah have to cut and prepare it himself? It's obvious that building the ark meant sacrifice for Noah, his wife, and his sons. They sacrificed their time, money, and reputations, but the rewards were worth it all. Lot was called upon to sacrifice as well. He was to leave his home and everything he owned in order to save his life. He obeyed, but a lack of obedience in his life preceding this monumental decision cost him dearly.

Stand firm in your faith. Noah was undoubtedly tempted to quit at least once. After all, he was surrounded by scoffers; it had never rained; and the whole idea of mass destruction . . . well, that just wasn't like God. He surely must have thought about how silly he would look with a boat in his back yard if it didn't rain. And what about his future? If he didn't get to work on something *productive*, he would never be able to retire. Thoughts like these must have occurred to him, but he chose to go against the tide for the sake of obedience. Lot's problem was that he was unwilling to stand alone. He wanted the fellowship of his neighbors, regardless of how vile they were, so he compromised. To live for Jesus in a corrupt world, we have to go against the tide. But we must also consider the cost of going *with* the flow.

Let your light shine. Pastoring a church in Las Vegas allows me to witness some of the most extraordinary light shows imaginable. The lights are remarkable but deceiving, for they don't reflect the addiction, lust, greed, and misery in the lives of those who are drawn to them. I've known Christian families that are much the same way. On the surface all looks nice, but inside they're falling apart. We need to allow God to cleanse us of our secret sins; to heal the hurts we hide; to conform us into His image so our lives reflect the perfect love of God. Only then will those around us be drawn to the Father of lights. (See James 1:17.)

Dedicate time to your children. Time is the currency of the 1990s; a precious commodity. If we're not careful, the *pressing* will demand it all and leave none for the *important*. All too quickly our children are grown—and we've missed it. Whatever it takes, we must make time to work, play, and *be* with our families. When the angels came to Sodom, they found Lot in the city gateway with his friends. When the flood came, Noah was with his family.

Set family goals. A common cause can mold a family into a focused team. It gives each member a reason to sacrifice and work hard. Whether it be a project around the house or a family vacation, work together to accomplish goals.

Pray for the love of Christ. Ask that His love would flow through each member of your family. Scripture gives an example of such a prayer: "May the Lord make your love increase and overflow for each other and for everyone else, just as ours does for you" (1 Thessalonians 3:12). When Christians walk in the flesh, their homes are no different than the homes of unbelievers. Unless Jesus lives within us, we are incapable of expressing the love the world needs to see in us. Ask God to make you a more loving parent. Ask that the fruit of the Spirit be evident in your life to everyone around you.

We can demonstrate the love of Christ in our homes in many ways: by mutual respect for every member of the family regardless of age; by physical (non-sexual) and verbal affection; by honest, open communication or "speaking the truth in love" (Ephesians 4:15).

FOLLOW NOAH'S EXAMPLE

We cannot build a healthy home by wishful thinking or resorting to prayer as a "last-ditch effort" when we're falling apart at the seams. It requires work, dedicated prayer, faithful service to God and, above all, desire. We have to set the example for our family; we have to separate ourselves from the world's way of thinking and its value system. This isn't accomplished by becoming a family of hermits, but by living in obedience to God's laws regardless of what those around us are doing. We're to be *in* the world, not *of* the world. Noah is proof that it can be done. If we follow his example, we'll build a healthy home in an unhealthy world.

The Reverend Paul Goulet is senior pastor of West Valley Assembly in Las Vegas, Nevada. He is a provocative speaker and author of the Reconcilers *series, a course that develops healthy leadership. As a pastor, counselor, and health care professional, the Reverend Goulet has had vast experience in helping individuals deal with a myriad of spiritual, psychological, and social problems.*

In the past ten years, Pastor Goulet has helped start several counseling centers in churches and served as director of Capital Counseling Ministries in Sacramento, California.

He is a graduate of Ashland Theological Seminary and an ordained minister with the Assemblies of God.

Paul and his wife Denise have three children: Isabelle, Christine, and Samuel.

3

Family Fundamentals

SAMMY VAZQUEZ

The foundation for the American home is crumbling, and parents of teenagers are begging for help. As a youth pastor and district youth ministries director, I counsel with scores of young people and their parents. More than ninety percent of my counseling is with families who lack the building blocks that make up a strong family unit.

Each November basketball coaches across America bring together a group of boys they hope to mold into a winning team. They condition them and drill them repeatedly on the fundamentals of the game, two hours every day for weeks. Finally, the opening game of the season arrives. The gymnasium is packed; cheerleaders are yelling; and the place is charged with excitement. Having played basketball, I know what's going on behind the scenes: the coach has gathered his team for one last lecture. He's done all he can do to physically prepare them. Now he must mentally charge them to go out and win. He says, "Fellows, we've worked hard over the past few weeks. We've spent hours on the fundamentals of this game, and I've drilled you on all the plays. I know you can win, but it won't happen by chance. You have to go out there and execute what you've learned."

As parents striving to build a strong family unit, we're not unlike the basketball coach. We nourish and train our kids day in and day out, year after year, investing our lives in them. In time, like the basketball coach who watches his boys run onto the court, we will watch our children enter the arena of adult life, knowing we've done all we can to prepare them physically, mentally, and spiritually.

I'll never forget the day I left home to take my first youth pastorate in Las Vegas, Nevada. Fighting back their tears, my parents said, "Sammy, remember the things we've taught you. You'll be a great youth pastor. We love you." I couldn't say a word. I just nodded, hugged them, and left. During the drive from Morgan Hill to the San Jose Airport, I reflected on the many "practice sessions" where the fundamentals of life were drilled into me by parents who loved me. Since then, I've reached back into my memory many times to draw help in raising our four children and building a strong family. Many fundamentals go into building a strong family unit, but I'd like to focus on four: love, affirmation, dealing with failure, and family activities.

TRUE LOVE

In his book, *The Man in the Mirror*, Patrick M. Morley tells a heart-wrenching story about an ill-fated Alaskan fishing trip. Four fisherman landed their small seaplane in a secluded bay where they spent a great day pulling in the salmon. They returned to their plane late in the afternoon only to find it high and dry because of the fluctuating tides. They had no choice but to wait until morning when the incoming tide would make takeoff possible again. The next morning, with the plane afloat, they started the engine and took to the air. Within minutes, however, the plane fell back into the sea. A leak had caused one of the pontoons to fill with water, and the extra weight caused the plane to crash. All four survived the crash and, after praying, decided to abandon the sinking plane and swim for shore, fighting icy waters and a vicious riptide as they went. Two of the fishermen were strong swimmers and, though exhausted, managed to reach the shore. The other two, a father and his twelve-year-old son, didn't fare so well. Cradling the boy in his arms, the father and his son were swept out to sea. This man, who could have reached the shore alone, chose to die with his son rather than leave him behind.[1]

Though we wouldn't hesitate if put to the test, most of us won't be called to make the ultimate sacrifice for our children. We can demonstrate how much we love them in other ways. One is by listening. If we don't make time to really listen to our kids, and especially our teens, we contribute to their problems. Parents who desire to build a strong family unit must pay attention and show interest in what their kids have to say; that includes hearing what they *don't* say as well. By not listening, we say we're not interested, and we lack genuine love.

We also express our love by the way we communicate with our children. About a year ago an angry young man came to me for counseling. After we chatted for a while I asked him, "What kind of relationship do you have with your parents?" Immediately he answered, "I can't stand my dad!" He told me of one incident after another where his father had embarrassed him, belittled him, and broken promises to him. He used the phrase, "the way he talks to me..." repeatedly. Finally he said, "I wish my father were dead. I can't wait to leave home."

The way we communicate with our children is vastly important to their self-image. If they are torn down, they'll have little regard for themselves—and less for us; but if they are built up, they'll have a positive self-image and will relate well with those around them. They'll have self-respect and will know how to respect others.

Discipline is another way in which we express our love. Scripture gives clear meaning and support for discipline:

> Foolishness is bound in the heart of a child; but the rod of correction shall drive it far from him—Proverbs 22:15, KJV.

> He who spares the rod hates his son, but he who loves him is careful to discipline him—Proverbs 13:24.

> The rod of correction imparts wisdom, but a child left to itself disgraces his mother.... Discipline your son, and he will give you peace; he will bring delight to your soul—Proverbs 29:15,17.

One hot summer day, my mother, sisters, and I were picking prunes. Being a typical boy, I thought it would be more fun to throw the prunes at my sisters than put them in my basket. My mother didn't agree. She broke a twig from a tree, took me behind a bush, and spanked me. After my tears subsided, she pointed to a newly-planted prune tree and said, "Do you see that long straight stick next to the tree? That's there to help the tree grow straight. The winds will blow and even gust at times, but that stick will keep the tree in line until it's big enough to support itself; without it, the tree would grow crooked. This twig," she said, indicating the one she'd whipped me with, "is like that stick: it will help you grow straight." I've never forgotten those words.

Living near Bethany College, I attend many of their basketball games. Coach John Block is a no-nonsense type of guy who has no problem expressing himself to his team. I've seen him pull players out of a game, strongly *suggest* they execute what they learned in drills the week before, then bench them for a while. When they go back into the game, they're ready to follow instructions. Sometimes our children, teens included, need a "time-out" when they violate their training. It's never fun to administer, but discipline is necessary if we truly love our kids.

AFFIRMATION

A poem entitled "A Life in Your Hands" offers great insight into the role of parenting:

> If a child lives with certain criticism,
> He learns to condemn;
> If a child lives with hostility,
> He learns to fight;
> If a child lives with ridicule,
> He learns to be shy;
> If a child lives with shame,
> He learns to feel guilty;
> If a child lives with tolerance,
> He learns to be patient;
> If a child lives with encouragement,
> He learns confidence;
> If a child lives with praise,

He learns to appreciate;
If a child lives with fairness,
He learns justice;
If a child lives with security,
He learns to have faith;
If a child lives with approval,
He learns to like himself;
If a child lives with acceptance and friendship,
He learns how to find love in the world.

Dorothy Law Halte

We affirm our children by recognizing that each one is an individual with his or her own talents and abilities. Parents should help them to see the difference they can make in their world, especially when submitting themselves to God. Study men and women of the Bible together, such as Joseph, Gideon, Esther, and Ruth, and discuss the ways in which they impacted their world. We can help our young people identify things they do well. Perhaps they're athletic or musically inclined. Maybe they have leadership or business skills. Whatever their ability, help them to develop it through the classes they take in school or through outside training.

By the same token, help them recognize their inadequacies. Don't allow them to cover them up or to make excuses for them. Instead, help them deal with shortcomings in a positive manner so they don't become a hinderance later in life.

DEALING WITH FAILURE

We've all heard it said: "It's not important whether you win or lose, but how you play the game." That ethic may have been accepted in the past, but our teens live in a world where winning is everything. Such a philosophy carries a tremendous burden. And the truth is we don't always win.

When I was in college I loved to watch Monday night football. My favorite commentators were Howard Cosell and Don Meredith. During a game Cosell said, "If only Stabler had seen Branch on the other side of the field, the Oakland Raiders would have scored a touchdown." Don Meredith replied, "If *ifs* and *buts* were candy and nuts, we'd all have a Merry Christmas." Someone once said, "Don't complain about the way the ball bounces if you're the one who dropped the ball." When we teach our children to live without *ifs* and *buts,* it helps them deal with failure so they can get on with life, and it keeps them from asking the wrong questions. Instead of asking, "Why did *I* drop the ball?" it's easier to ask, "Why were my friends disloyal?" "Why was the teacher unfair?" "Why do they always blame me?" "Why don't they understand?" "Why did the coach cut me?" The blame is always on someone else. As parents, we must encourage our kids to admit when they "drop the ball" instead of complaining about how it bounces. If handled properly, failure can be a tremendous tool for Christian growth. We don't win in life by never making mistakes; we win in life by learning from them.

FAMILY ACTIVITIES

We've all heard it said: Today is the first day of the rest of your life. We'll never have a better opportunity to spend time with our families. There are no insignificant moments or experiences; each day counts. I heard the story of a researcher who, in studying the history of the Adams family, came across the diary of Charles Francis Adams. On a certain day, the only words recorded were: "Went fishing with son. Day wasted." The entry in the son's diary was a little different. He wrote that the fish were not biting, so they passed the afternoon in conversation. Brooks, who was twelve at the time, asked his father many questions and his dad explained the many aspects of life. Later, Brooks recalled, "It was the most significant day of my life."[2] There are no insignificant events, no wasted hours when we spend time with our families.

The "family vacation" has almost become a thing of the past. Time is a precious commodity and there never seems to be enough of it. Families can still spend fun and relaxing time together, building a strong and lasting relationship. Here are some ideas:

Go for a bike ride. Plan a fifteen or twenty mile ride, pack a lunch, and go for it! Your local bike shop should have information on bike paths and offer ideas for a family outing.

Head for the beach. There are plenty of things to do once you get there. You can swim, build sand castles, play frisbee or touch football, and barbecue burgers. After dark, it's great fun to build a bonfire, roast marshmallows, and share memories of the past and dreams of the future. If you don't live near an ocean, a lake will serve just as well.

Go to a major league baseball game. If you're not near a city that hosts a team, most cities have a single, double, or triple A farm club. You don't have to buy expensive seats, and you can take your own lunch or dinner along.

Go camping. This great American activity can be very inexpensive and very relaxing.

Take your kids to lunch. Pull them out of school periodically (preferably one at a time) and take them to lunch. There's nothing like one-on-one interaction to get to know your kids.

Pull out Monopoly or Trivial Pursuit, or any of your favorite board games.

Head for the mall. Mothers and daughters are especially fond of this. And if all you buy is caramel corn, that's okay.

Plan a night at the movies . . . right in your own home. Make it a double feature with Jerry Lewis and John Wayne. Throw some popcorn in the microwave oven and enjoy!

Crafts. Try your hand at models, needlepoint, puzzles, whatever strikes your fancy. My wife Terri still enjoys times when she and her mother can work on crafts together.

Devotions. Spending time in family devotions is a pleasant, rewarding activity, even for teenagers. Invariably, what was meant to be a ten-minute devotion ends up an hour or more in our house. One question leads to another and, before you know it, the evening is gone. Family devotions are not only enjoyable, they're eternally rewarding.

The Bible says our children are a tremendous blessing from God. When we work in unity with Him to build a strong family unit, there is no greater calling in all the world.

The Reverend Sammy Vazquez is Youth Ministries Director for the Assemblies of God Northern California/Nevada District. He graduated from Bethany College with a B. A. in Biblical Studies, and is working toward a Master's from Southern California College.

He and his wife Terri have four children: Kristi, Kandice, Sammy III, and Nathaniel.

4

Better Family Communication

NORM SCHULZ

Conflict is an inevitable part of family life. Families will always have conflict, particularly during the adolescent period. During these years our teens are dealing with physical and emotional changes, as well as struggling with identity, authority, and responsibility. Parents rarely face a day without conflict and stress. Thus, we often hear comments like: "Just wait until you have teenagers. They won't be cute and cuddly forever. Once your kids become teenagers, your house will never be the same." Such comments leave little room for optimism, but take heart: these years can be very rewarding.

Learning how to deal with conflict is an essential part of family life, but it requires time and commitment. Results of a recent Gallup survey of American youth revealed more than twenty-five percent of teenagers don't discuss their day's events with their parents. More than forty percent hadn't received a word of praise from their parents; fifty percent hadn't received a hug or kiss; and fifty-four percent hadn't heard the words "I love you" during the survey period.

Family conflict can drain the life and joy out of our homes, but conflict is not to be feared. When understood, it can result in growth for us and our teens. From an international survey, Dr. Dudley Weeks listed the most frequently used responses to the word "conflict." They were: anger, avoid, bad, control, destruction, fear, fight, hate, impasse, loss, mistake, pain, war, and wrongdoing.[1] It's obvious that conflict is perceived as a negative experience. But, in itself, conflict is neither positive or negative. The way we *respond to* and *deal with* conflict is what's negative or positive. With the right attitude and the Lord's help, conflict can be constructive.

COMMON MISUNDERSTANDINGS

When we lack an understanding of conflict, misconceptions occur, and they can hinder the resolution of the conflict. Four common misconceptions are:

Conflict is a sign of poor family relationships. This misunderstanding causes parents to feel insecure and lowers self-esteem. It can make us believe we're poor parents if conflict occurs and causes unnecessary worry and anxiety. The truth is, conflict does occur. We must learn to anticipate it before it happens, deal with it immediately, then rejoice in its absence.

Anger is always destructive and negative. Anger, one of many human emotions, is *not* always negative. The difference is in the attitude in which we display our anger.[2] Attitude is one of the most important decisions we make each day. Properly directed, anger can bring resolution and a positive end to conflict.

If left alone, conflict will take care of itself. This tends to be the most popular way to deal with conflict, but it's not the most effective. Occasionally, time will diminish conflict, but it seldom resolves it. Often, feelings reappear at a later date and at an escalated level of conflict.[3]

Conflict must be resolved now. This is a solution-driven response, but it doesn't allow for flexibility or a multiple step solution. It makes us believe conflict must be quickly "fixed," which can result in the illusion that everything is fine. This too can repress emotions that will appear more intensely later on.

IDENTIFYING LEVELS OF CONFLICT

Parents and teens end countless debates, arguments, and conflicts without properly identifying the seriousness of the disagreement. If we can identify the level of conflict, whether it be the result of poor communication or blatant rebellion, it will help us know how to deal with the problem. Successful resolution is the ultimate goal, which will turn the potential destruction of conflict into a learning, growing experience.

Poor communication. Conflict that results from poor communication is a common occurrence in everyday life. It can simply be a misunderstanding of what is communicated, which is easily resolved; or it can be the intentional withholding of information between parents and teens. When we withhold information from our teens (i.e., not fully explaining our requests; giving "do-it-because-I-say-so" orders), we cultivate frustration. By the time our kids reach their teens, we should communicate more fully when we give them responsibilities, when we impose restrictions or limitations on their social life, when we require certain attitudes and behaviors. When we explain the reasons behind our actions, rather than just dishing out orders, we give them a chance to understand our decisions. By explaining all sides of the issues, we give them a part in decision-making, which is vitally important as our kids move toward adulthood.

When our teens withhold information from us, they cultivate mistrust and suspicion. We want to know "what they're hiding" when they may simply lack the right words to communicate; they may not yet be ready to share; or perhaps they're seeking more independence. If we recognize this, we'll be less apt to *react* and more willing to *respond*.

We must do everything possible to keep communication open between us and our kids. Our ability to communicate—and communicate well—is essential to our effectiveness as parents. We must be good listeners, learning to hear what our kids are saying verbally and *non-verbally*. It's important we "hear" their frustrations, doubts, fears, and concerns, even when they're not expressed. Statistics suggest that many teenagers value their friends above their parents. If that's true, perhaps it's because they're able to communicate with their friends without condemnation or anger.

Aggravation and irritation. Everyday we face situations that cause aggravation and irritation. These are generally minor incidents that can be overlooked and don't have an effect on the overall relationship between us and our teens. But should the incidents escalate and become increasingly repetitive, they need to be addressed; otherwise they can lead to a decline in the parent-teen relationship. It's possible that an increase in minor irritations can be symptomatic of a larger, underlying problem.

Battles. Conflict at this level is more intense, more serious, and can be described as a "win-lose" situation. When a teenager disagrees with his parent in a given situation, he will often be more interested in his personal benefit than the good of the family. It's common for heated arguments to occur at such times. The teen will often bring up past mistakes or broken promises, and often the accusations will be intense and exaggerated. It requires additional patience on our part to keep the situation under control. We must stay focused on the issue, separate the problem from the person involved, and not resort to personal attack even if the teen does.

To diffuse conflict at this level, we should approach the situation with *resolution* as our goal; not victory. We must set the tone, striving for a controlled, non-antagonistic atmosphere. If we must delay confrontation to achieve this, that's okay. In discussing the conflict, avoid generalizations: be specific. Look for areas in which both parties agree, and use them as a starting point. Compromise where possible, but do not violate your standards to do so. When that happens, nobody wins.

Conflicts in which battles occur are almost unavoidable, especially with teenagers in the home. Don't feel like a failure, or like you're losing control because they occur. Learn how to face them responsibly, and they can result in growth for everyone involved.

Rebellion. Rebellion, which is characterized by outright disobedience, lack of respect, and disregard for standards and values, can negatively influence other siblings. This is a level of conflict from which nothing good can result. It must be dealt with swiftly and firmly. Once again, it's important to separate the behavior from the individual, regardless of how personal the rebellious teen becomes.

Generally, at this level there are no "quick fixes." As in all areas of conflict, prayer is essential to a positive outcome. God, who is as desirous as we are to resolve the problem, provides wisdom and insight when we pray. Beyond that, we must lovingly, but firmly, address the behavior and get to the underlying cause. We must be willing to see it through to the end no matter how hopeless the situation may seem. Too much is at stake to write off a son or daughter. We shouldn't nag them, or allow hard feelings to brew beneath the surface, and we should never be afraid to discipline them.

It's important to focus on getting a rebellious teen through the difficult time. They need our unconditional love and acceptance. It may be necessary to recruit reinforcements to help us deal with rebellion. Pastors, youth pastors, counselors, friends in whom we trust and who are respected by the troubled teen, can all lend assistance. Proverbs 12:15 says, ". . . a wise man listens to advice."

UNDERSTANDING CONFLICT

Parents and teens may look at the same situation and see things differently. It's like putting on a pair of glasses that aren't our own: things look out of focus. In the same way, we can't expect our teen to see clearly through *our* glasses, or from our viewpoint. They have an entirely different perspective. We need to try to understand each conflict from our teen's perspective, and try to help them understand ours. We can't expect them to naturally see the situation in the same light we do. Once again, the importance of communication cannot be understated.

When trying to understand our teen, we might ask the following questions:

- What are the needs of my teen?
- What has led him to think or behave as he does?
- Am I listening to and understanding what my teen is saying and meaning?
- What vulnerabilities (areas that will trigger negative responses) does my teen have, and what can I do to avoid them?

When trying to understand conflict, we might ask these questions:

- What is the conflict about?
- What is it *not* about?
- Am I sure this conflict is with my teen and not with myself?
- What have I done to contribute to the cause of the conflict?
- Is this conflict a single event that shows no consistency with the rest of the relationship?
- Is this conflict the latest in a series of conflicts showing a problem with the relationship as a whole? If so, what needs to be done to improve the relationship?
- What are *my* vulnerabilities, and how will I deal with them?
- What needs to be the outcome of this conflict?
- If the outcome is different than what I want it to be, what damage or impact will that have on the relationship?[4]

Understanding these areas as they relate to conflict can be a major step in resolving them.

LOOKING TO THE FUTURE

In working through conflicts with our teen, we should focus on the present and learn from the past. Memories of a conflict that got out of hand can be a roadblock for dealing with present conflict. We must not let the past impede us in our efforts for the present. As we and our teen grow in our ability to deal with conflict, what happened in the past doesn't have to happen now.

Ways to learn from the past:

1. Remind our teen (and ourselves) of the enjoyable times we've had together. We're not enemies; we're moving toward positive resolution *together*. This will help us face the current conflict more favorably.

2. Look at past conflict and determine what skills were (or would have been) helpful in resolving the conflict quickly and effectively.

3. When in conflict, remember other conflicts have been resolved. Remember how we grew and learned through them. It should help us be able to work together in resolving the present conflict.[5]

A POSITIVE ATMOSPHERE

Atmosphere is the framework on which we will agree, disagree, and strengthen the relationship with our teen. We need to be aware of the atmosphere we establish by our attitude as we confront conflict. Here are some ways to ensure a positive atmosphere. We should:

1. Select a time that is free from interruption and is sufficient to complete the discussion.

2. Select the best opportunity for concentration and clear communication. For example, if it's late at night and everyone's tired, it might not be the best opportunity for achieving positive resolution.

3. Select a place that is non-threatening and won't allow anyone to be embarrassed. Teens are very self-conscious. We must deal with conflict privately, and never try to embarrass them in front of their friends.

4. Establish a feeling that "we're dealing with this together."

THE DON'TS OF CONFLICT

Don't get involved in a power struggle. This will only sabotage our efforts. Experts agree as power increases, authority decreases. To avoid power struggles, we should not argue. It only wastes time and fuels the conflict. We should not approach conflict with the idea that we must "win." Positive resolution requires that everyone wins.

Don't become detached from the conflict. Don't allow business or anything else to diminish our passion to be close to our families. A minor conflict may not seem important to us, but it may consume the thoughts of our kids.[6] We must be sure to resolve every conflict to keep communication open and our relationships solid.

Don't blame. Attaching blame intensifies the problem and hinders resolution. Seldom does conflict rest solely on the shoulders of one person. We must all be willing to acknowledge our contribution to the conflict and get onto the solution.

Don't make it worse than it is. Our emphasis must be on resolution. We delay that when we exaggerate the problem or bring other issues into it. We need to deal with the issue at hand without magnifying it, throwing around insults, and letting our feelings get out of control.

THE POSITIVE SIDE

The foundation of a Christian home is Jesus—even when there's conflict. Though frustrating and, at times, painful, conflict can produce growth in everyone concerned. If we learn to deal with it in a Christian manner, not only will our home be a happier place, but we'll prepare our teens to victoriously face a world that's filled with conflict.

The Reverend Norm Schulz, an ordained minister with the Pentecostal Assemblies of Canada, served as youth pastor in Canada from 1983 to 1989. Since then, he has served as missionary evangelist to Eastern Europe with a focus in Romania and Albania.

Pastor Schulz, a graduate of Northwest College, is currently working on his Master's.

He lives in Lynden, Washington with his wife Lynn and their two children: Brandon and Brittany.

5

The Single Parent

SCOTT HAGAN

Baby boomers know Opie Taylor—the Huck Finn of early television. Opie was part of America's first nationally known single parent family. His mother had died and he lived with a single father and great aunt. Modern America's single parent households are much different than the one portrayed on "The Andy Griffith Show." Today's single parent family, for the most part, is the result of divorce or an out-of-wedlock pregnancy. Indeed, the Taylor home would represent a small percentage of the single parent families of the 1990s. For instance, Andy Taylor would be replaced by a father consumed with his career and personal fulfillment. Instead of seeing his father respectably date the Pollyanna of the local diner, Opie would be wondering who that woman was spending the night with Dad, and why it wasn't the same woman as last month. Oh, Opie would never ask, but he'd watch; he'd wonder and, eventually, emulate.

In today's family, there wouldn't be an Aunt Bea. She'd be too embroiled in her own problems; she wouldn't have room in her life for Opie or Andy. With her weekly Alanon group meeting and her latest horoscope warning her not to take risks, Aunt Bea wouldn't be much help to the family. Thus, today's Opie would have to find support and friendship elsewhere, perhaps with a neighbor in his apartment complex named Barney—someone willing to pay attention to the boy and give him an occasional pat on the head. But, typically, today's Barney has been married and divorced himself and has his own set of problems and emotions monopolizing his time.

Today's Opie has a parent overcome with confusion. As a result, his life is filled with one obstacle after another and little optimism. He is disconnected from grandparents and other family members, related only by stories of the past. His city is filled with violence and schools that pursue political agendas over principles. With no leadership or structure in his life, he turns to the streets for direction, the byproduct of a dysfunctional family.

CONFUSION: THE NEW CORE VALUE

America is finally becoming aware of the startling statistics on the plight of the family. Most believe there is little hope for the family—especially in the inner city—as it suffers from moral decay, devoid of Judeo Christian values. Scholars theorize why this has occurred and offer myriad solutions. But little progress is made in reversing the trends that have led to the decline.

The menagerie of definitions for the family has merely served to stifle solutions to America's family crisis. When hundreds of definitions of the family are conjoined to hundreds of agendas for what the family should be, it's the equivalent of trying to put together a jigsaw puzzle with no interlocking pieces. When it comes to progress, to solutions, to putting the pieces together, the quest results in endless fumbling. This, in essence, is a picture of government or education trying to resolve the crisis of the American family. Endless fumbling. Nothing works because there are no absolutes. It's every man for himself. Every definition is acceptable. Every agenda applauded. This works well for getting elected to public office, but it does little to help America's dysfunctional families.

GOD'S VIEW OF SECULAR DYSFUNCTION

If you're a single parent, you're not on the outside of God's wonderful principles. Your situation is close to His heart, and He's there to guide you through your journey. He wants you to experience freedom and complete joy.

What is a dysfunctional family? It's a family that is not functioning the way God designed. Dysfunction has more to do with fractured attitudes than with fractured structures. A first-marriage husband and wife with 2.8 children can have dysfunctional *attitudes*, even though the structure appears functional. Likewise, a single parent in a fractured structure can see proper Christlike attitudes prevail in the home. This is not to say God isn't concerned with the family structure. He designed it to be a man and woman married for life, raising their children in the way of the Lord. But God is able to take a fractured structure and create a redemptive environment.

Dysfunction can represent historical failure or present destruction. Dysfunction is a buzzword everyone is running to hide behind to explain the family mess. What should be the Christian's response? Does God speak to our past? To our immutable history? To the parts we can never change?

First, our past generational failures *explain* our weaknesses; they do not *excuse* them. People by the tens of thousands are allowing their first family to destroy their second family. The popular view of dysfunction is that the actions of my parents will greatly affect my actions as a husband, wife, mother, or father. They feel as though they are trapped or doomed. If Dad was an alcoholic, then I will be an alcoholic who beats my kids. Or, I'm a witch today because Mom was an astrologer. Christians should not be wiled by this philosophy.

In Mark 7:14-16, Jesus gave us the "Law of the Tea Bag." He taught that it's the flow of the heart that darkens our life. Nothing that enters a man from the outside can defile him. Have you ever noticed what happens when you place a new tea bag in a cup of clear, hot water? As you swirl the tea bag back and forth, the clear hot water turns bleak and dark. Soon, the surroundings screen out the tea bag. Visibility is zero. It looks exactly like the people who stumble day after day into counseling offices. Their surroundings are bleak and visibility is at zero. This causes a longing for a new surrounding, a new start, a new *anything* to help them escape the darkness.

Many orchestrate a new surrounding: they dive into a fresh cup of hot water and enjoy the view for a while. Then something begins to happen. The bleakness creeps back. Soon visibility is back to zero and the frustrating life-cycle of a fresh start gone bad is back again. This is dysfunction in all its glory.

Dysfunctional people never realize present surroundings are the product of present content. They are ruined by the current flow of the heart. The hot water of life draws out the beauty or pain of the heart. So, overcoming the wrenching philosophy of "dysfunctional attitudes" begins with understanding how the human heart works and what Jesus came to actually do for us. Jesus came to grant heart transplants.

Scripture teaches that we are "born again" of an "incorruptible seed" (1 Peter 1:23, KJV). Physical conception begins with the "seed" of life from our parents. That process has become the scapegoat for our problems. Dysfunction claims that our problems are linked incurably to our first birth. However, if salvation represents a "new birth" from the "seed" of our heavenly Father, shouldn't that "seed" have enough power to overcome the "seed" of an earthly father? The "seed" represents the qualities of the parent from whom it flows. It contains tendencies and traits that affect our lives. But that is precisely the power of salvation, of becoming "born again." The qualities of our Father in heaven now live in us and desire to transform us into the likeness of Jesus. The motives, reactions, attitudes, outlooks, and responses of Jesus are all contained in that "seed." No one can claim the power of salvation and still claim that their earthly parents hold the key to their future. Scripture teaches us that "whom He foreknew, He also predestined to become conformed to the image of His Son . . ." (Romans 8:29, NASB).

Before fanaticism sets in, let me restate that our earthly parents will forever in this life brand our existence. I used to chuckle at my dad for the way he would fall asleep on the couch and awaken after the nightly news with a jerk. As he rose from the couch, it was clear rigor mortis had set in. Bent over, he would literally wobble down the hall to bed. As a boy, this scene made me mumble, "Get in shape, Dad. You look terrible."

Two months ago, I too fell asleep on the couch. Awakening with a jerk, I felt an unusual stiffness throughout my body. Feeling the need to compensate for my awkward steps down the hall, I too set off for bed. Suddenly, I caught a full-bodied reflection in the window. I knew I had seen that person somewhere before. That unique, bent-over position, the waddle, hmm . . ., "Oh my heavens, it's my father!" Right away I did ten jumping jacks. Twenty years later, the apple hadn't fallen far from the tree. The less I am physically around my father, the more I become like him in so many ways. This is all part of God's wondrous design. But this is a far cry from the bondage people allow in their lives by denying the power of God and believing a deception about the power of their past. Salvation represents a freedom from your sins and the sins of the preceding generations. The Christian cannot use his past as an excuse for the present. Sadly, the popular view of dysfunction is becoming the accepted view of the Church.

I extend to all parents—single, divorced, widowed, or discouraged—to consider the Christ who lives in you. When Christ suffered on the cross, compromising nothing, obedient to the very end, something powerful unfolded. The veil of the temple was torn in two, the earth shook, and the skies darkened in an eclipse of the sun. This phenomena paled in comparison to the experience of a nearby centurion. To say Jesus looked like a champion or a hero in this moment is to deny history. Yet, the centurion realized what the miracles and healings were saying all along: "Surely, this is the Son of God!" He was overcome by a loving God who willfully clothed Himself in every imaginable garment of suffering, who willingly endured the cross. This is so paramount to understanding the steps you will need to take to deny the deceitful side of living with a "dysfunctional attitude." The cross represents much more than an act that assures forgiveness. Jesus took on your sin, your parents' sin, and your grandparents' sin in order to break sin's long historical reign. Being a Christian means sin is no longer calling the shots in your life. Its dominion has been broken and defeated. When Jesus has been made your King, sin can no longer take peace from your heart and impose its consequences on your life. Though your family history may relentlessly flash before your eyes, "Greater is He who is in you than he who is in the world" (1 John 4:4, NASB). Once you come to grips with how God views dysfunction, you can move on to the vital atmosphere of success for the family.

AN ATMOSPHERE OF FORGIVENESS

Forgiveness is an atmosphere as well as an act. Single parent families will be given opportunity at every turn to integrate bitterness into their way of life and thinking. When money crunches or repairs mount, the small voice of bitterness will begin to whisper its doubts. When father-son campouts roll around, so can the frustration. When circumstances only a mother or father can address become reality, helplessness and despair take residence. Can the single father understand how to deal with his daughter's first period? Can the single mother confront pornography or masturbation in her thirteen-year-old son? What happens when a daughter has no father to walk her down the aisle? A spouse may forgive the occurrence of divorce or death, but what will fend off bitterness when these situations occur? The key is living in an *atmosphere* of forgiveness. Survival and success depend on learning how to forgive like Jesus forgave.

Jesus modeled forgiveness on the cross. Christians have become so familiar with the cross that they have forgotten its significance. The rejecting world never sees or studies the cross; it is irrelevant to the unbeliever. Yet those six hours contain more practical advice than "Dear Abbey" could give in ten lifetimes. Jesus went to the cross without a script in hand. The human side of Jesus interacted with the earthly condition surrounding Him. His work on the cross was sincere. Bitter Christians, however, act as though Jesus died in a hole at midnight while wearing camouflage instead of upon a hill in broad daylight. The events of the cross were lit up brighter than the neon lights of the Las Vegas Strip. There is no excuse for any Christian to miss the potency of the cross.

Picture Jesus hanging upon the cross those six hours, dying . . . "while we were yet sinners" (Romans 5:8, KJV). On your worst day—on that day—Christ was dying for you. While the murderer was murdering and the rapist raping, Christ was dying for them. His blood dripped on those who played Lotto for His clothes. It was then He uttered, "Father, forgive them; for they know not what they are doing" (Luke 23:34, NASB). Single parent families must learn Jesuslike forgiveness if they wish to overcome the past.

Only by applying two concepts that Christ displayed on the cross can you walk in peace in any relationship, no matter how complex the situation. First, Jesus forgave quickly. The wound was fresh and the blood still flowing when He cried, "Father, forgive them" (Luke 23:34, NASB). How unlike the forgiveness we see modeled in society: we love to wait until the blood dries, then scabs and scars. Most of us calculate the damages and measure our forgiveness accordingly. With Jesus, forgiveness flowed as quickly as His blood. This is Jesuslike forgiveness. When pain strikes through an unhappy memory, think of Jesus and forgive. When overcome with loneliness and the burden of responsibility becomes too great, picture Jesus and forgive. When there is no father to walk you down the aisle, visualize Jesus and forgive. Forgive quickly. Abandon yourself to God and never trust your scars.

Second, Jesus forgave thoroughly, ". . . for they do not know what they are doing" (Luke 23:34, NASB). Unforgiveness is the process of trying to make someone understand the impossible. Could the centurions and soldiers have ever understood the depth and ramifications of their actions that day? It would have been useless to try to make His executors understand the cost of their deeds. Jesus did not hinge His forgiveness upon their understanding. He released them, realizing they could never understand.

Trying to make a father understand the pain you endured when he abandoned his family years earlier will only deepen your hurt; his lack of understanding will only further frustrate you. Try to be like Jesus who released people quickly, as well as thoroughly. People rot their souls in the vain pursuit of vengeance, forgiving only when convinced the wounding party understands their actions. Single parent families can save their futures by heeding the works and words of Jesus—not only with the major turning points of your history but also beyond every turn that lies ahead. Breathe deep into your lungs the life-giving forgiveness modeled by Jesus and serve notice on your past, present, and future. Regardless of anyone else, your life can be marked by quick and thorough forgiveness.

Single parent families can become a mighty influence on society. As people see God working through their lives and in their attitudes—thriving, not just surviving—it will awaken others to the power of God and make Jesus irresistible to those in need. Moses, Joseph, Daniel, and Timothy impacted nations. They each allowed something greater than their history to guide their lives.

Single parents, be encouraged with your standing before God. Do not view God's help through others as a second rate deliverance. God can provide role models for you and your children. Be spiritually cognizant of the power you possess as a link in the family chain. Four generations from now, should Jesus tarry in His return, a small child will be sitting with a young parent and asking questions about Jesus. He might say, "Daddy, how come Jesus is so important to you?"

"Well, son, my mommy and daddy took the time when I was a boy your age to make sure I knew how much God loves me. They learned it from your great-grandma and great-grandpa who also faithfully served God. They became Christians because your great-grandmother had a mom who was the first to become a Christian in our family history. She had a horrible life at the beginning. Her husband beat her and eventually left her for an awful addiction to alcohol. She and her daughter—your great-grandmother— began attending church a long time ago. As best we can tell it was because of them that we know Jesus and love you today."

Sound like a fable? Not a chance. I think you get the picture.

The Reverend Scott Hagan is pastor of The Harvest Church, a thriving ministry in Laguna Creek, California. He graduated from Bethany College and spent seven years in youth ministry before pioneering The Harvest Church in 1990. Pastor Hagan is a frequent speaker at camps and writes "Captain Dad," a question and answer newspaper column.

He and his wife Karen have four children: Joslyn, Tyler, Kramer, and Spencer.

RELATIONSHIPS

The better part of one's life consists of his friendships.

Abraham Lincoln

6

Peer Pressure: The Unfriendly Fire

DONNIE MOORE

There's a fire burning out of control—an unfriendly fire that is destroying many of our children. This fire has smoldered for a long time, but now it's out of hand and is blazing in the lives of our youth. It's the fire of peer pressure.

The term "peer pressure" sounds harmless when compared to words like crack-cocaine, gang-violence, unwanted pregnancy, rape, satanism, and murder. But peer pressure is a major issue in today's generation of teens. A fourteen-year-old girl came to me after a church service in Napa, California. She was a pretty girl; her parents were involved in the church; and she was a regular part of the youth group. She told me some of her "friends" had described to her how great it is doing drugs. They said, "It's awesome! We can't describe it; you've got to try it." They were talking about LSD. A week later, in a different city, a junior high student named Lisa shared that her "friends" at school told her she could become popular by sleeping with one guy at school and then telling everyone.

Not long ago, I listened as a young man described his activities of the previous weekend. He went to a party and got so drunk he started throwing up and eventually passed out in his own vomit. His "friends" took him home and left him on the front porch where he spent the night. When I asked him why he'd done that, he said, "I wanted to be accepted by my friends." Today, it's not only drug dealers that young people have to say no to; often it's their best "friend."

This past year, after a Christmas program at a California Youth Authority prison, I asked a young man about a tear-shaped tattoo on his face. He said it signified he had murdered someone. I don't believe he really wanted to kill anyone, but he *desperately* wanted to be accepted by his "home-boys." To be accepted, he had to "accomplish" something. I've found that youth gangs are not normally comprised of kids who are inherently violent; they're simply willing to risk anything to be one of the guys.

Most of us underestimate how important peer approval is for our young people. These days, if teens are *not* having sex, if they're *not* partying, if they're *not* using drugs, including alcohol, their peers pressure them to do so. Peer pressure says you have to wear *this* label and *these* shoes; you have to conduct yourself in *this* manner; your reputation depends upon it. Kids steal and risk going to jail to get a pair of designer jeans or tennis shoes with the "right" name on them.

And the pressure doesn't come from only peers. The media adds another dimension to the problem. For example, television and movies portray Christians as nerds, as people who are "out of it." They portray the church as irrelevant and outdated. By watching the news and reading the paper, one might easily think all preachers are crooks.

Many secular rock musicians—particularly heavy metal performers—take it a step further. Their message is: "If you want to be somebody, you'll live the way we tell you to live: do drugs, have sex, don't believe in God, rebel against your parents, and stay away from church." This is the type of media pressure kids face every day. Many are willing to throw their lives away just to find acceptance by those around them.

There's a fire that's burning.

That precious girl in Napa would risk blowing her mind on acid and drug addiction so her friends would not be displeased with her. The young man at the California Youth Authority was willing to end a life so he'd be accepted. Lisa was willing to give her body away at thirteen and, because of heroes like Madonna, would throw modesty aside and wear lingerie to school.

Many of our young people today have chosen the approval of their peers over concerns that their sin will bring God's judgment. But they're willing to face the displeasure of God rather than that of their friends. They're also willing to go against their own conscience and personal conviction in exchange for the temporary peace they find in the acceptance of others. Why are they willing to compromise their beliefs to conform to the standards of their peers?

THE CAUSE

What causes our young people to surrender to peer pressure? They fear rejection. They've seen it happen to others, and they don't want it to happen to them. No one likes to feel insignificant, inadequate, or like an outcast. So they conform to keep from losing their place in the crowd. Cliques are an example of this; they're built out of insecurities and are fueled by racism, economic status, or the fear of rejection. That's why members of cliques feel threatened by outsiders: their position in the clique is jeopardized by them.

I recently spoke at an awards banquet for Franklin High School athletes. After the banquet, when report cards were handed out, I asked a young man named Tim about his grades. He said he'd gotten As and Bs in all his classes. His friends, who were standing around, laughed at him and then bragged about their Ds and Fs. I was amazed. I couldn't believe they'd laugh because Tim got good grades. I turned to him and said, "Let them laugh; one day they'll all be working for you."

COUNT THE COST

Followers should find out where the crowd is going because there's a price to pay for following the wrong crowd. They must understand the first time they make a mistake or don't perform to the crowd's standard they lose their approval—along with peace of mind, contentment, and their sense of satisfaction. Striving for the acceptance of others deprives our young people of self-fulfillment. Any acceptance they find will be elusive and fickle. Here today; gone tomorrow.

As an example, I was a quarterback on my college football team. I remember one game in particular where I completed a fifty-yard pass to win the game. I'll never forget the sensation as the fans erupted into cheers. But the very next week I didn't play as well. The same crowd who cheered me the week before booed me off the field. I learned a great lesson: if you live your life for the applause and acceptance of the crowd, life will be an emotional roller-coaster: up one day, down the next. When our youth build their security on the approval and acceptance of their friends, they face certain turmoil.

If your children live for the acceptance of their peers, challenge them to ask these questions:

1. Am I willing to suffer the consequences of my actions in order to gain the acceptance of others?
2. What must I do in order to keep that acceptance?
3. What have I gained because of that acceptance?

If they realized they won't see ninety percent of their graduating class once they leave school, would it still matter who was better dressed? Who was better looking? Who was more popular? The acceptance that drove them to make the wrong decisions won't matter anymore. There will be no profit in having won the temporary acceptance of their peers only to lose the approval of God.

We all want people to like us, but how much are we willing to sacrifice for their approval? We must set the example for our kids. We must be more concerned with what God thinks of us than what man thinks, or we run the risk of being like the religious leaders that Jesus spoke about: "Nevertheless among the chief rulers also many believed on him; but because of the Pharisees they did not confess him, lest they should be put out of the synagogue: for they loved the praise of men more than the praise of God" (John 12:42,43, KJV). God never ordained that we find self-worth by pleasing others. We are accountable to Him alone. And when we stand before Him, we will stand alone.

God is not impressed with anyone's fame, glory, achievements, or influence. Scripture says, "All men are like grass, and all their glory is like the flowers of the field. The grass withers and the flowers fall, because the breath of the Lord blows on them.... The grass withers and the flowers fall, but the word of our God stands forever" (Isaiah 40:6-8). God is not affected by the unfriendly fire of peer pressure, because He has no peers. He bows to no pressure; He has never played to the crowd. He has allowed the world to exist, knowing the majority of those He created would reject Him. But His standards don't change, regardless of what the latest popularity poll indicates. He has no one to explain to, account to, apologize to, or appeal to. He is God.

DEADLY DECISION

Darwin Benjamin, a close friend of mine at the University of the Pacific in Stockton, California, played running back on our football team. As quarterback, I often handed the ball off to him and watched him run. It was exciting to watch him on the field. But Darwin was more than a good runner; he was an encourager. I was having a bad game when we played the University of Miami. I completed more passes to the cheerleaders than I did to my teammates. I heard boos from the crowd, but Darwin encouraged me, saying, "You can make it, Donnie; don't quit."

I hadn't seen Darwin in seven and a half years, but I'd heard rumors he was dealing cocaine and his life was really a mess. I hoped I would run in to him sometime. One night I was speaking at a church, preaching a message on the Father-heart of God. I gave an opportunity for people to respond at the end of my message, and many hands went up. As I looked over the crowd I thought I recognized one of the men whose hand was raised. I thought it might be Darwin, but I wasn't sure. As I looked closer at the upraised hand, I knew it had to be him. The little finger on his right hand had been injured and was noticeably crooked. I'd seen it many times lifted in the air when he scored a touchdown or when I handed off the football to him. It was Darwin all right, but he was no longer the well-built running back he'd been in college; he wasn't the handsome "ladies' man" he'd been then, either. Drugs had almost destroyed him.

Darwin found acceptance all his life through sports. If he did well on the field, people would like him. In high school he was an all-American running back. In fact, he scored the first touchdown his team had made in fifty-nine games. Unfortunately, because of his athletic ability, his academic problems were overlooked. Teachers told him, "Hey, Darwin, don't worry about the test Friday. Just go out and run the ball Friday night."

Although he graduated with tremendous football accomplishments, his grade point average was below 2.0. Universities throughout the United States were recruiting him, but because of his grades only the University of the Pacific would take him, and that was on probation. But when he got to UOP everything changed: all the attention and publicity he'd received in high school was gone.

He began to feel a tremendous void in his life, and he desperately wanted the attention and recognition he had in high school. Many of his college teammates began to get letters of intent from the NFL, leaving Darwin embarrassed and ashamed. He decided to do whatever it took to regain some attention. He tried to get the girls his teammates couldn't, even if he had to deceive them to win their trust. Then he took advantage of them to impress the guys. It didn't take long for the women to catch on, and his reputation took a dive.

When he left college he started going to nightclubs. It wasn't long until he found his drugs brought him friends. The cocaine and crank he offered made him popular. When the clubs closed at 2:00 a.m., Darwin invited everyone to his house where they would party all night. Once again people knew who Darwin was; but for all the wrong reasons. Drugs brought him everything money could buy: cars, jewelry, fine clothes, and the popularity and recognition he craved.

He had a girlfriend named Yolanda with whom he would party and do drugs. When she became pregnant they continued their reckless lifestyle, never giving a thought about what drugs might do to the baby she was carrying. Eventually they went to a doctor to talk about the pregnancy. A sonogram revealed that Yolanda was pregnant with twins. Nevertheless, they continued doing drugs.

When Yolanda was about to give birth, she was rushed to the hospital in an ambulance. As complications set in, Darwin was nowhere to be found. He'd put on his gold jewelry and fine clothes, loaded his pockets with money, did a few lines of cocaine, and was about to leave for his favorite club when Yolanda's mother called and asked him to drive her to the hospital. Reluctantly, he agreed. I've experienced the birth of two daughters, and it's difficult to imagine a father not wanting to be present at the birth of his child. But drugs had made Darwin numb to the real issues of life, like they do to everyone who falls into that trap. They'll take you further than you're willing to go; they'll cost you more than you're willing to pay; and they'll keep you longer than you're willing to stay.

As Darwin walked into the hospital waiting room, the doors swung open and a doctor approached. "You must be Mr. Benjamin," he said. "We need to talk." Yolanda had given birth to twin girls. One was born perfectly healthy;

the other was not so fortunate. She had an aneurism of the brain, her left side was paralyzed, her head was swollen, she had a cyst from the back of her neck to her lower spine, and her intestines were outside her body.

When Darwin reached out to touch his little girl, she lifted her hand and took hold of his finger. She squeezed it as if to say, "Help me, Daddy, please help me." He knew the drugs they'd used had caused his baby to be born in such a horrible condition, and he began to sob. He knew his gold jewelry and money wouldn't help him now.

After keeping the newborn five days in an intensive care nursery, the doctor said they had to see if the baby could live without a respirator. They wrapped little Natasha in a blanket and placed her in her father's arms. She struggled for every breath. Darwin wept as he told her how sorry he was for what he had done to her. He told her he was going to get his life together; he was going to change. She opened her eyes, looked directly into his, then gasped her last breath and died. Darwin couldn't deal with the guilt and the shame. He went back to drugs—this time to escape the pain.

Two years passed before a friend invited my former teammate to hear me speak. Darwin had been raised in church. Yolanda's parents were pastors. Something inside told him if he could reach me, he would get the help he needed. That Sunday night, he heard about Father-God and opened his heart to Christ.

Darwin made a promise to Natasha that her death would not be in vain. Consequently, today he speaks to more than one hundred thousand teenagers each year in junior and senior high schools and youth prisons. He willingly shares his story so others can be spared his pain. No longer a hundred and fifty pound drug addict, Darwin is considered one of the top gang counselors in California, and the high school assembly program we conduct together received the Delinquency Prevention Award in that state.

Parents, sit down with your children and tell them Darwin's story. Review with them the key points of this chapter. Listen to what they are saying. Be their friend and take time to show a genuine interest in their lives. Talk to them about what the world's music and movies are really preaching. Teenagers are making the most life-controlling decisions at a time in their lives when they're least qualified to make them. Help them make the *right* decisions and you'll help extinguish the unfriendly fire of peer pressure.

The Reverend Donnie Moore is the founder and director of Radical Reality, an evangelistic ministry aimed at the youth of America. He was saved in 1982 while attending the University of Pacific in Stockton, California, and started a Bible study with five students. In four years it grew to three hundred, and the college ministry that began with that revival has spread to many Northern California college campuses. Radical Reality also travels to high school campuses in the form of an anti-drug, anti-gang, pro-abstinence assembly and received the California Youth Authority Delinquency Prevention Award of the Year from the Governor's Policy Council on Drug and Alcohol Abuse.

He is also chaplain for the Oakland A's baseball team. Each year he has the opportunity to speak to every team in the American League and has seen many professional athletes accept Christ as their Savior.

Donnie and his wife Cindy have two children: Brooke and Anna.

7

Choosing a Mate

PAUL OLSON

In France, a gypsy woman shatters a clay pot in front of the man with whom she wishes to live and will remain with him for as many years as there are pieces of the pot. When the time expires, they may separate or make another contract by breaking another pot. Until recently in some agricultural communities, a peasant woman could not marry until she proved her fertility by either giving birth or reaching an advanced stage of pregnancy. Conversely, in Brazil a girl who lost her virginity had little hope of marriage. In many parts of the world, fathers still have an undisputed right to sell a daughter to the highest bidder, with virgins almost always commanding the highest "brideprice." In some societies marriages arranged by parents are still commonplace. In Japan, "three-day rent marriages" are not uncommon. The bride-to-be is escorted to the bridegroom's house by her parents. If the couple likes each other after three days, a formal wedding follows;

if not, the relationship is quietly dissolved without embarrassment to either party.[1]

Should parents be involved in helping their children choose a partner for life? After all, it's one of the most important decisions they'll make. If so, is there a biblical basis for such involvement?

MARRIAGE AMERICAN-STYLE

The blind bliss of two young people madly in love makes me shudder. As I meet with couples for premarital counseling, I try to pass on the experience of couples married for more years than the ones I'm counseling have been alive. I try to get them to understand how complex marriage is, and warn them about the pitfalls. Invariably, they're more interested in the number of counseling sessions "required" than in the content of those sessions. Typically, they enter premarital counseling certain of two things: that they'll marry each other, and that their marriage will succeed because they're so much in love.

When counseling couples, I always ask: "Have you come seeking help in deciding whether you should marry each other, or do you just want help in preparing for marriage?" A few have indicated they would postpone their wedding, but I've never had a couple say they would cancel it if I thought they shouldn't marry each other.

Do couples really understand what they're doing when they say "I do" on their wedding day? I doubt it. How can a person twenty years of age adequately anticipate the challenges of loving an incomplete, imperfect, changing spouse when they're incomplete, imperfect, and changing themselves? How can they truly understand the implications of sharing the joys and woes of parenthood, the dwindling and rekindling of passion, the stress of finances, the wonders of intimacy, the fears of growing old? They can't. The few years of life they've experienced haven't prepared them for such things. At best, marriage is an adventure with an unpredictable future.

PARENTAL INVOLVEMENT

Many cultures firmly believe parents are more qualified than their children when it comes to choosing a life partner. Since ours is not one of them, what can we do to help our children succeed in marriage? Several passages of Scripture provide guidelines we can use to help our children select a mate. In writing to the Corinthians, the apostle Paul gave instructions for marriage. He was speaking of a widow remarrying, but the principles can also be applied to a single person contemplating marriage for the first time. He wrote, "She is free to marry anyone she wishes, but he must belong to the Lord" (1 Corinthians 7:39). Two significant principles can be observed from this passage. The first principle declares an individual is free to choose his or her own mate. The second that, as a Christian, they must select a mate who is also a believer. Proverbs 18:22 affirms the first principle, saying, "He who finds a wife finds what is good." The young man is not *assigned* a wife; he *selects* her. In 2 Corinthians 6:14, the second is affirmed: "Do not be yoked together with unbelievers."

Parents need to make sure their children understand they will be free to make more decisions for themselves as they mature. As children, they can decide what they want to eat at McDonald's. Later, they can choose their own clothes, classes, and friends. Ultimately, they'll select who they will marry. By instilling the scriptural mandate for Christians to marry other believers, parents are doing the most important thing they can to help their children have a successful marriage. The following steps will help parents ensure their children follow biblical guidelines in selecting a mate:

Start early. Most parents, if they get involved in the mate-selection process at all, get involved too late. If you haven't instructed your child in the importance of marrying a believer, it will be too late when they fall in love with an unbeliever. Long before they reach their teens, begin saying things like: "Someday you will choose someone to marry. It's most important that you choose someone who loves Jesus as much as you do." Assure your child that he or she has plenty of time before making such a choice, but look for every opportunity to address the issue.

Emphasize their freedom to choose. As the child gets older, say things like:

> I want you to have lots of friends and date lots of different people. When it comes time for you to choose a mate, it will help you make a better choice. The choice will be yours, but I want to help you gain the experience to choose well. Don't be in a hurry. Make sure you've done the things that are easiest to do while you're single, like finishing college, job training, traveling. When the time comes for marriage, I hope you'll seek my counsel. I'll not interfere in your choice as long as you choose to marry a Christian.

Prepare your child to fall in love "head first." As your child approaches the teen years, talk about your role in helping them find positive friends and in building healthy relationships. Ask them questions such as: "What do you look for most in a friendship? What makes you want to be with one person more than another? What do you dislike enough to not want to be around a certain person?" Such questions will help them think about relationships, become intentional in their friendships, and not leave them to chance.

In the earliest stages of dating, parents can encourage their child to make a list of characteristics they value in another person and characteristics they want to avoid in the person they would date. Teens should continually be counseled to settle for nothing less than the best, rather than dating someone just because they show interest in them. This will help the child to thoughtfully limit the field of those eligible for a love relationship. It's far better if the head proceeds the heart in matters of love.

Downplay the idea of "falling in love." Sooner or later, every young person will "fall in love." Parents need to help their teens put the experience of falling in love into perspective. Describe, from your own experience, what it feels like to fall in love: sweaty palms, "butterflies," weak knees. Be honest and detailed; acknowledge how real it is, and how powerful and exciting. But make sure your child understands that the kind of love we fall into can easily be fallen out of. Explain that falling in love is like parachuting out of an airplane: at first there's a great adrenaline rush, then a period of blissful flight. But sooner or later, the ground of reality rushes up to meet you. How you land depends on how well you're prepared to handle the rush and then the drift. It can be so much fun you want to do it over and over again, but it takes a different kind of love to make a lasting relationship.[2]

PREVENTING A BAD CHOICE

What should a parent do if, against all counsel, their child chooses to marry an unbeliever? First, continue to counsel your child, using the Word of God as your authority. Arrange for someone you know who has made a similar choice to share with your son or daughter. They'll undoubtedly offer advice to think twice before entering such a marriage. Pray for your child's future mate. Ask the Lord to bring a godly man or woman into their life. If you see them begin to date or fall in love with an unbeliever, bombard heaven with your prayers. God is as concerned with their choice as you are. Do whatever you can to prevent an unequally yoked relationship.

I've told my children if I see them falling in love with an unbeliever, I'll do everything in my power to prevent them from making a choice they'll live to regret. If necessary, I'd quit my job and move to another state or country to break off the relationship. If they were away at college I'd cut off their financial support to prevent an unhealthy choice. If they were living away from home I'd fast and pray for the relationship to be dissolved. I'd never resign myself to letting them make such a decision in the name of "personal choice."

Any young person who sincerely desires Jesus to be Lord of their life will not resent such behavior from their parents. If the seeds of positive parental guidance are sown early and with care, the fruit will be forthcoming.

The Reverend Paul A. Olson earned his doctorate in family studies and marriage counseling from the University of Minnesota. In addition to his counseling practice, Paul served as Director of Family Ministries for seven years at First Assembly of God in

Helena, Montana. Most recently, Dr. Olson established Family Strategies, a non-profit ministry noted for its School of Marriage church curriculum. He has had several family-related articles published in Christian magazines and has published a book, The Distinctively Christian Marriage.

He and his wife Kathryn have two teenagers: Katie and Caleb. They live in the Elkhorn mountains near Helena.

8

Searching for Heroes

SCOTT GOSSENBERGER

More than ever, teenagers need heroes who will show them what it means to be a man or woman of God. They need heroes who find their joy in serving Christ and whose excitement for the Lord is infectious. Yet, the trend of the American church has been to emphasize education as a means of leading individuals to a committed life in Christ. Even Pentecostal churches that traditionally placed an emphasis on experience have begun to emphasize the informational side of Christianity. Many contend you can *teach* someone into the faith. That may be true for a few, but the vast majority, especially the young, will come to know Christ through personal experience. That's not to suggest pure doctrine isn't important or the Bible isn't the ultimate authority for our lives. Rather, discipleship must take on a more relational approach.

In his book, *Of God and Men,* A. W. Tozer wrote of the Church:

> The talk is that we need revival, that we need a new baptism of the Spirit—and God knows we must have both; but God will not revive mice. He will not fill rabbits with the Holy Ghost. . . . She must repudiate the weaklings who dare not speak out, and she must seek in prayer and much humility the coming again of men of the stuff prophets and martyrs are made of. God will hear the cries of His people as He heard the cries of Israel in Egypt. And He will send deliverance by sending deliverers. It is His way among men.[1]

Young people need mentors, heroes who will lead them on a spiritual journey filled with personal encounters with the Lord. Without them, many of our young people will be at risk of spiritual death.

We need those who will challenge us to live our lives for Christ; those who will share their lives so we can catch their intensity for Jesus.

Heroes have always been an important part of my life and ministry. I was raised in a strict, pentecostal home. Movies were strictly taboo and television only partially accepted. My parents monitored the programs I watched to be sure I wasn't exposed to violence and immorality. I wasn't even allowed to watch "Batman," which was all the rage. Once my parents caught me watching it and restricted me from television for a week. There was, however, one exception. John Wayne movies were not off limits. He became my hero and inspired me to want to be a hero, too.

Rather than take the bus, I rode my bike three miles to and from school during my freshman and sophomore years in high school. During those bike rides I would daydream that I was a hero of heroes, fantasizing that I single-handedly saved Southern California from a Russian invasion. I even imagined myself rescuing a girls' camp from would-be rapists.

I remember one heroic dream in particular: Our family attended Melodyland Christian Center in Anaheim, so that was the setting. While sitting in an evening service, absorbed in the pastor's sermon, a group of communist terrorists, armed with machine guns, entered the building and encircled the congregation. The leader pushed our pastor off the platform and told us we were all going to die because we were Christians. I managed to slip through a door that led to the sound room. I was the only one able to escape the building because, after all, I was the hero of the dream. As with most fantasies everything worked out perfectly. It just so happened I had taken my motorcycle and .22 caliber rifle to church that night. I started my motorcycle and headed straight for the front of the church. Just before reaching the glass doors I pulled a wheelie and busted through them, and, in the process, knocked off two of the terrorists, firing at the others as I rode around the back aisle of the church. Bullets were flying everywhere and terrorists were dropping like flies, but, of course, I didn't get shot. Only the leader was left. He took aim and shot at me as I rushed the platform to take him out. Wounded, I fought through his barrage of bullets and fired a shot that ended his life. This dream occurred about the same time I developed a crush on a girl named Sheila, whose feelings for me were not the same. So, lying on the platform with blood flowing out of me, the whole congregation rushed to the front and began to cry for me. Sheila pushed her way through the crowd, knelt over me, and cried uncontrollably. In a faint voice I asked her to come closer, then said these unforgettable words: "Sheila, you should have loved me while I was alive."

Naturally, the church erected a monument in my honor while Sheila had to live with her loss.

The heroes who inspired my dreams were important because they challenged me to expect more out of myself. Today's heroes generally fall into two categories: athletes and entertainers. Both should be appreciated for their talents, but problems develop when individuals are admired for their talent alone. The recognition they receive may give them an opportunity to be a positive influence in the lives of others; however, the talent should be secondary to the influence. In other words, they should be admired most for bringing about positive changes in others.

Our society places too high a value on talent. In school the ones who get the most attention from teachers and peers are the ones with recognizable talent. Colleges spend millions of dollars to recruit star athletes who will make them shine. On a local level, kids will pass around the sports page when it highlights young people from our youth group while those who minister in a hospital may go unnoticed.

COMMITMENT

Christian heroes can challenge teens to seek a higher level of commitment to Christ. According to Lawrence Crabb, people have two basic needs: to be loved for who they are, and to be significant to someone. When entertaining talents are elevated above character, those who lack such talents feel insignificant and insecure. Such feelings will drive most young people in one of two directions: either they will withdraw into themselves or they will find some activity, even if it is morally wrong, that will gain them recognition.

Significance that comes from achievement is usually short-lived and, for most, unattainable. Young people need heroes who are touchable, who model character that is attainable. Professional athletes and entertainers are often poor heroes because they're *un*touchable, and their level of ability is *un*attainable for most young people. Touchable heroes who are everyday people challenge us to excel beyond mediocrity. Today's teenagers have had their potential held captive by a society that has set a false priority of talents over character. We need to introduce our young people to heroes who, by their character and lifestyle, will challenge them to a greater commitment to Jesus. Young people need heroes who will live a godly life in front of them.

At the age of twenty I knew God had called me to youth ministry, but I was deeply insecure about my ability to perform as a youth pastor. I'd been a late bloomer in high school, beginning my freshman year at 4'11" and weighing ninety-five pounds. Football was definitely out, so I joined the wrestling team. I lost every match. I also joined the marching band and made fifth-string as a trumpet player. As a sophomore my counselor told me I wasn't smart enough for college so I should prepare to get a job instead. My junior year the steer I was raising for my agriculture class died, and I got fired from my job. My senior year . . . well, I graduated.

Things started coming together when I completely committed my life to Christ, but I carried a lot of insecurities from past failures into my new life. About that time our youth group got a new youth pastor named Jerry Hanoum, who took a special interest in me. He often took me out for a soda or invited me into his office to talk. I admired Jerry and enjoyed our times together. I saw in him qualities I wanted to emulate. For his part, Jerry believed in me enough to give me meaningful responsibilities in the youth group and trusted me with ministry. It meant a lot to have someone, besides my parents, believe in me.

One night, Jerry invited me over to his house just to hang out. Naturally, I accepted. That night Jerry and his wife Yvonne laid hands on me and prayed for God to guide my life. I'll never forget what Jerry said to me after he finished praying: "Scott, I believe God sends youth pastors one young person who will change their world if that youth pastor will pour his life into the one God sends. For me, you're that person." That one phrase—spoken sincerely by a man I respected—changed my life. He taught me that "I can do all things through Christ who strengthens me" (Philippians 4:13, NKJV), and challenged me to live a life fully committed to Christ.

BETTER CAUGHT THAN TAUGHT

Young people need heroes like Jerry because Christianity is better *caught* than *taught*. The strength of Christianity is not so much in its information but in its ability to change lives. If asked, most teens will say they find the Bible boring. Their attitude toward God's Word is the result of looking at it simply as a source of information. To them it's a textbook. But if they approach it with the understanding it brings life to those who read it because God speaks directly to them through it, they will have a love for Scripture. They'll best learn this truth by observing heroes who have a love for the Bible.

The same principle applies to Christianity. Most young people don't feel that the "spiritual" parts of our faith, such as prayer, Bible study, and church attendance, are exciting. As a result, the majority of teens in our churches are immature Christians who only fill pew space. They need to learn these things give life as well, but, once again, this is best learned by emulating heroes of the faith.

Occasionally I conduct seminars for youth workers. I start by hanging signs throughout the room with names of famous athletes, entertainers, and religious figures. On one sign I write the name *Jesus*. I begin the seminar by asking the leaders to stand under the name of the person with whom they most identify. Rarely does anyone stand under the sign with the name *Jesus*. This illustrates that people don't identify with Jesus; instead they identify with Him as He is incarnated in the life of a particular believer. It's a mistake to train young people to be *academic* Christians. Jesus transformed the world because He poured His life into a small group of people. They were changed by His life and they, in turn, changed the world with their lives.

If our young people are going to change the world rather than be changed by it, they need godly heroes. Parents who are concerned with the spiritual growth of their children need to find a hero who will invest in their child.

PROFILE OF A CHRISTIAN HERO

Heroes are everyday people who, by the power of God's Spirit, do supernatural exploits. They can be found in any church. They don't wear white hats and aren't usually conspicuous, but you can find them if you know what to look for. They're the ones who spend time at the altar: the ones who know how to pray. They support the church and the pastor with their words and their deeds. They come for the work days as well as the potluck dinners, and they teach Sunday school or drive a bus. They're faithful to God and to His kingdom.

Heroes invest in people. Five years ago I left Southern California to be the youth pastor of a church in Vacaville, California. There I met a man named Bob who would become one of my closest friends. When I first met him I wasn't particularly impressed by his potential to minister to youth. He often came to the youth meetings in his work clothes, covered with paint, dirt, and sawdust. In my opinion, he wasn't the best candidate for a hero, but I had a lot to learn.

Bob came to every youth group event and gave himself to the young people in his group. The kids nicknamed him "Daddy Bob." Though he had five children of his own, he often invited kids from the youth group to his home. He would pray with them, answer their questions about the Bible, and let them just hang out with him. He loved them and they loved him, and he was able to significantly impact their lives. In only three years, our youth group grew from thirty to 450 kids, largely because of Bob.

Bob could have spent more time building his contracting business or enjoying recreational activities, but his priority was investing in people. Heroes of the faith understand the only things we can take with us to heaven are the people we've touched with the love of Jesus. If you need a hero for your children, find someone who invests their resources in people.

Heroes are servants. Serving isn't limited to feeding the homeless or visiting convalescent homes. People serve in a variety of ways. I have a friend who felt prompted by the Lord to serve his church more diligently, so he got a scrub brush and cleaned every toilet in the church one Saturday. Dr. George Wood, whom I worked under, served his congregation by spending twelve to fifteen hours preparing for each sermon. In the five years I was there, even while studying for my master's degree, I learned something new and spiritually significant from each sermon.

Serving is the most basic of heroic qualities because no one is considered a hero for being selfish. It's only when we reach out to others that we have an impact on the world around us.

Not long ago I watched on the evening news a group of people who spent several days and thousands of dollars to save some whales that were trapped in ice. A tremendous amount of energy and emotion went into that rescue effort, and those involved were heralded as heroes. In turn, heroes of the faith are those who will serve others with the same kind of intensity that went into saving the whales so that they might be delivered from the bondage of sin and born into eternal life. Those are the kind of individuals our children need to observe.

Mark Buntain, missionary to India, was a servant-hero. When I first heard him speak, I was moved more by the passion with which he spoke about his work among the people of Calcutta than I was his words. He spent his life in one of the most impoverished cities in the world. He built a hospital for their sick bodies and shared the love of Jesus for their sick souls. It was apparent that he loved those people and would serve them faithfully as long as he lived. I was deeply challenged the night I heard him speak. When he called for those who would commit their lives to missionary service to go forward, I went. I didn't respond because I felt called to foreign missions but because I wanted to be a man like Mark Buntain. Mark was a hero to those who knew him and to the entire nation of India. I've discovered that finding a hero is easy when you look for someone who serves.

Heroes are admirable in all areas of life. Heroes are people who possess admirable qualities, but not everyone with admirable qualities will invest in the lives of our young people. You may know someone who has been faithfully serving in the Sunday school program at your church for fifteen years. That's a wonderful example of faithfulness to service. But if that person neglects or abuses their spouse, it nullifies their positive influence potential. A few months ago someone donated a tennis bracelet to a retreat ministry of which I am the president. The bracelet was made from separately purchased gems. It had green stones with diamonds in between and looked like a nice piece of jewelry. I was excited about selling the bracelet and putting the money toward our retreats. My excitement turned to disappointment when the jeweler said the bracelet had little value because quality stones had been used with low grade stones. The same principle applies to people who influence our kids. While we all have flaws, heroes included, we must have consistency in our walk with God to be of any real value.

Some years ago I was the youth minister in a church where the sanctuary also served as a gymnasium. Every year the youth group sponsored a church basketball league, forming teams from several churches in our community. The idea was to have fun and fellowship, and most of the time that was the case. When you put competitors together, however, sometimes the fellowship is lost in the quest to win. Our pastor, an excellent athlete who had played baseball and basketball in college, had a natural talent for any sport he tried. He was also a charismatic speaker and completely dedicated to his congregation. He had a powerful prayer life that challenged me to be more faithful in that area of my spiritual walk. But his desire to win often brought out the aggressive part of his personality, and he would sometimes have to apologize for his behavior. Even so, that flaw didn't negate his more admirable qualities. I still considered him a hero and a person I wanted to emulate.

Heroes are not perfect; they're not flawless. They're people who occasionally fail. But they admit their failures and commit them to the Lord for His help. Only Christ was perfect. Nevertheless, we have heroes, like the apostle Paul, who have not achieved perfection but who "press on toward the goal for the prize of the upward call of God in Christ Jesus" (Philippians 3:14, NASB).

Heroes sacrifice all for the sake of the call. On May 21, 1843, a group of 875 men, women and children left Independence, Missouri to travel to Oregon. Some rode horses, others rode in wagons; at least half traveled the 2,200 miles on foot. They knew the journey would be difficult, but the promise of a rich new land was worth the effort. They knew they risked losing their personal belongings to raiding Indians and their loved ones to sickness. Yet they were willing to sacrifice all they had and endure incredible hardship in order to reach their promised land. They led the way for a half million others who would make the same trip over the next twenty-three years. Their successful journey populated the Northwest and nullified Great Britain's claim to the territory. Those trailblazers are American heroes because they gave all to make their dreams come true.

Some Christians share that same spirit of adventure. They're willing to make incredible sacrifices in order to accomplish their dreams. Like the settlers, they sacrifice the comfort of their old lives for the promise of a better one. They're convinced nothing short of an intense relationship with Jesus will satisfy them. They take Matthew 10:37,38 literally:

> Anyone who loves his father or mother then me is not worthy of me; anyone who loves his son or daughter more than me is not worthy of me; and anyone who does not take his cross and follow me is not worthy of me.

CONNECTING HEROES WITH OUR KIDS

The most obvious and accessible heroes for young people are their parents. I hope you're challenged to be the model God has called you to be. Most young people admire their parents, though they usually don't say so. When I ask kids who their heroes are, they don't usually name their parents, but when I ask who they most *admire,* they usually name one or both. The reasons for their admiration are varied, but most agree on their parents' dedication to them and to God.

As children reach the teenage years they often look to people other than parents for role models and heroes. It can be threatening when our children admire someone other than us, but when we understand it's a natural part of the growth process, we can help provide responsible substitutes. Don't be afraid or jealous if your teenagers want to spend time with their youth pastor or a friend's parents. Recognize that everyone will benefit when the values you wish to impart are reinforced by other adults. My son is four years old and still thinks I'm the greatest. But there will come a time when he'll look to others as he tests his independence. As long as I ensure he has someone Christlike to influence him, I have nothing to worry about.

Young people need to be discipled by adults who are committed to Christ. Many churches have youth pastors on staff who disciple their young people. But churches that operate their youth outreach with volunteers can also have a discipleship program. What's important is that the youth ministry of your church makes discipleship a priority.

The most effective type of discipleship is one that is relational. Most programs stress curriculum and homework, feeling if you get them reading, writing, and praying enough, it will stick. But most young people do what it takes to get through the discipleship program, then when it's over they don't apply what they learned. A discipleship program that is *relational* is one where leaders share their life in Christ with the kids. Obviously, the strength of such a program depends on the strength of your youth leaders, so choose them carefully.

Young people commit themselves to Christ when they have an experience with Him. As a teenager I went to every youth camp. They were fun as well as providing an escape from the responsibilities of home and school. They were also a chance to find the girlfriend of my dreams. But those weren't my only reasons for attending camp. At every camp I attended, God did something supernatural in my life and in the lives of my friends. I looked forward to camp because I knew I would experience God there. It was at camp that I committed my life to Christ, was baptized in water, and filled with the Holy Spirit. We often criticize the mountaintop experience, but they're important. Such experiences affect young people for eternity. They become spiritual landmarks that help them make the right choices later in life. Camps and youth retreats are critical to the discipleship of our young people. They are investments worth every dime we spend.

If your church doesn't have a youth program, or if there isn't a viable discipleship ministry operating within the youth program, you may want to find someone in the congregation to get involved in your teen's life. Include them in some of your family activities. Have them over for dinner or go to a restaurant after church. Let the entire family develop a relationship with the mentor so everyone is working toward the same goal.

Whether discipleship takes place within the youth ministry or informally by an adult, it must be intentional. It's not enough to just be a friend. The relationship must be focused on leading young people into a personal, powerful experience with Jesus.

Several years ago I received a letter from a girl in my youth group named Rainy. Her letter helped determine my priorities as a youth pastor. She wrote:

> My thoughts of you are so unspoken. I've never really said how much I appreciate what you've done for me. I never gave a clue to how much you touched my life. You've set such a perfect example of what I wish to be. You're so kind and patient; I see the Holy Spirit in your eyes. You helped lighten the path to our Lord above. I realize now that I will serve my life in loyalty and witness through my joy and love. It's special people like you that make life worth living for. You help us understand that everything will be all right if we let the Lord lead the way. You've taught us all so many uncountable things, and we will always remember your name when we pray. You've been blessed in such a way that you teach our Father's Word so we can understand. So many were once lost and you showed them the way. There is so little you ever demand. You helped us cope with a world so cold. Sometimes it seemed there was only hating and lies, but somehow your messages seemed to make it all better. Maybe you're an angel in disguise.

Rainy was in the hospital when I first met her. Her mother had recently died and her father lived out of state, so she lived in her mother's house with her sister and a family friend. I was asked to visit Rainy by her neighbors who attended our church. At the end of my visit I asked if she wanted to receive the Lord. With tears in her eyes she prayed and asked Jesus into her life. I visited Rainy at the hospital several times and continued to encourage her faith. Weeks later she began to attend the youth group and rarely missed a meeting. She was special because I had shared her pain and emotionally invested in her life. I knew God had made our paths cross at a critical time. Her letter revealed how important I was to her and how God used me to communicate His love. Six months later I moved to Northern California. I often thought of Rainy and prayed for her, but I hadn't seen her for three years. Then I moved back to Southern California to pastor a small church. One Sunday morning, much to my delight, I saw her sitting in the congregation. When we talked after the service, I learned she was still serving the Lord faithfully. I always wanted to be a hero. Maybe I am to her.

The Reverend Scott Gossenberger graduated from Melodyland School of Theology in 1982 with a B. A. in Biblical Studies, then received his Master's in Church Leadership from Southern California College.

Pastor Gossenberger served as a youth pastor from 1981 to 1991. He began his ministry at Melodyland Christian Center in Southern California, spent five years at Newport-Mesa Christian Center, then moved to Northern California where he served at Vaca Valley Christian Life Center for three years. He has seen his youth groups grow numerically and spiritually by implementing campus prayer groups, outreach and discipleship programs, and evangelistic mid-week services.

He then pastored Bethel Assembly of God before moving back into youth ministry at Ventura First Assembly of God. He is also president of Youth Ministries, Unlimited, a youth worker training ministry.

He and his wife have two children: five-year-old Jason and two-year-old Jessica.

9

Resolving Conflict

KELLY S. GOINS

It was another hot, sticky Oklahoma summer day. Relatives were visiting, and for some reason I thought it was my chance to misbehave. Mom's warning looks had gone unheeded, so she said, "Kelly, if you do that one more time, you're getting a whippin'." Well, I did it—whatever *it* was—one more time; what followed was an event I would remember the rest of my life. Mom kept a *well-used* switch above the head molding in the kitchen. She grabbed it as she marched me out to the garage, but this time something was different. Mom didn't look angry; she looked hurt. She said, "Kelly, I've tried to be a good mother to you; I don't know what else to do." She handed me the switch and said, "This time, you whip me." Her eyes filled with tears and her chin quivered; and, for a brief moment, every whippin' I'd ever gotten flashed before my eyes. I remembered the time I threw the kittens against the barn to see if they would land on their feet; the Sunday afternoon I painted Indian markings on my face with iodine; the time I tricked the girl down the street into eating dog manure. They all came back to me. Now *I* had the switch; it was my turn to get even. But as I looked into her eyes, something inside me broke, and the whippin' came *my* way—in the form of love. It was the worst one I ever received—and without one blow of the switch.

LEARN TO CONFRONT

It's not easy being a parent, and sometimes it scares me to death. Since my daughter isn't even a year old, I haven't had much practice, but I wonder if I'll be strict enough, or sensitive enough, or *everything* enough. One thing I do know, regardless of what kind of parent I am, at one time or another, I'll encounter conflict with my child . . . and the outcome will be determined by how *I* handle it.

Every parent goes through conflict with their teenagers. If you haven't, you will. But don't worry: without a battle there would never be a victory. And though unpleasant, conflict can be ultimately good—if it's treated properly. When my mother was diagnosed with cancer a few years ago, we were devastated. Surgery was necessary and, though painful, successful. Today she has a clean bill of health. The cancer was unpleasant, but good came out of it because of what God did in our lives in the process. Conflict can be regarded in the same way. You can let it grow, or you can deal with it; but be assured it won't go away by itself.

Too often we ignore the problems we see in our kids. Maybe we're afraid we'll lose them if we confront it, or maybe we're afraid we'll expose the inconsistencies in our own lives. Whatever the reason, if we don't deal with the problems, they'll grow like a cancer. Left untreated, cancer brings death.

As parents, it's easy to blame other people for the conflicts we have with our children. We blame teachers, youth pastors, their friends, even ourselves. But positive parenting demands we allow our children to be responsible for their actions. The following article is an example why:

> **June 1967:** Daniel's just tired. He's always fussy when he's tired. I think all babies are. It's not his fault, poor thing.
>
> **April 1969:** Daniel just had a shot and his arm hurts. Kids always act up after they've had a shot. If you ask me, the nurse was a little calloused. It certainly isn't Daniel's fault.
>
> **January 1970:** I think Daniel's a little feverish. He looks flushed. Kids are difficult to manage when they have a fever and don't feel well. Maybe he has a sore throat too, because he just wouldn't eat his lunch—except his pudding.
>
> **March 1971:** Well, you must realize that Daniel is full of curiosity by nature. He's never seen a toy like that before, so naturally he wanted to investigate it. I'm certain he didn't mean to grab it from your child so roughly. Daniel is a very spontaneous child. I personally think the more you make out of something like this, the more harm you do.
>
> **July 1972:** I'm sorry about your sofa. We'll pay for the damage, of course. But things like this are to be expected with a highly spirited child like Daniel. Of course, I'd much rather have a spirited child than one who's just passive about everything. Children can be made that way, you know, if you stifle their activity.

September 1974: Well, obviously a child is going to fight when he learns that other children don't like him! What do you expect? I realize Daniel is quite strong for his age. We'll take care of any medical bills, even though I don't feel it's our responsibility—given the circumstances. I think it's a shame that people are blaming Daniel for this whole incident—and outright lying when they say he started it! He wouldn't do such a thing. That's not the way he's been raised.

May 1976: I realize what Daniel said was improper, and running from the classroom was not appropriate behavior. He feels just terrible about it, poor thing. He was almost in tears. If I may say so, I believe you're forgetting *your* role in this. When you callously return a test on which a child has gotten a *forty-seven percent*, you can expect some reactive behavior, especially from a sensitive child like Daniel. And at least Daniel's grade was *honest*. He informs me that the higher grades were gotten by cheating, and Daniel wouldn't do that!

August 1978: No, I'm sorry but it must have been some other boy. Either that or your daughter is on some vendetta against Daniel. My son would never say things like that to a girl. Why, I'm sure he'd blush if he even heard those words.

November 1979: Yes, I'm aware that Daniel is behind in his assignments. Of course he's behind. You give these ridiculous punishments for not having homework and then the child has double work to do. If he made up all that work at once, he'd have no recreation time at all. As a teacher, you certainly know how important it is that we let the children have time just to be children. Really,

I've just about had it! We experienced this same lack of understanding at Daniel's previous school. I'm beginning to lose faith in our educational system.

July 1980: Gang? Did I actually hear you say gang? That's the most absurd thing I've ever heard! Gangs are made up of juvenile delinquents! What do you think Daniel is? He's really just a child. This is positively insulting, and I don't intend to stand here and listen to another word.

October 1982: Listen, I'm going to say this just once. Daniel is not involved. I just spoke with him, and he was not involved! My child may not be perfect, but he does not lie to me. I'm sick and tired of this constant harassment.

February 1983: They all experiment with it. It's simply part of the culture these days, and there's no getting around it. As it turns out, this is the very first time Daniel has ever touched marijuana. He told me he was merely curious and didn't even like it. I know my Daniel. Now that his curiosity is satisfied, he won't do it again. He's not like those kids who take it all the time and turn into druggies. As far as I'm concerned, this whole thing is over. I see no point in dragging it out any further.

May 1983: Now why are we making such an ugly commotion over this? It happens to many children. And it's quite understandable. Here we have a impressionable young boy who's trying hard to make friends. The friends suggest going on a lark of sorts, to steal a little something insignificant just for the . . . I beg your pardon? It most definitely was *not* Daniel's idea. That's an outright lie! I know my boy, and he does not think like that. We intend to

reimburse the store for everything, of course. Daniel needs us to stand behind him now more than ever.
November 1985: Your honor, I'd like to say that this whole thing is a huge misunderstanding. In a very real way, it wasn't Daniel's fault. I happen to know my child very well and . . .

Author and Source Unknown

When faced with conflict in our homes—whether it's between us and our child, or our child and someone else—what do we do? Do we close our eyes? Do we run away from it? Do we blame other people? Conflict caused King Saul a lot of trouble because he didn't handle it well. When challenged by Goliath, he was paralyzed with fear, so God brought a shepherd boy in to do what Saul and his army couldn't. (See 1 Samuel 17.) The conflict he created in David's life was devastating—to David and to the people of Israel. Ultimately, it cost Saul the kingdom. He would have been better off dealing with Goliath instead of hoping he would go away. Remember, like the cancer, conflict has to be dealt with or it's destructive. If left untreated, it will destroy the fiber that holds a family together.

You say dealing with conflict is difficult and painful. You're right. And there's no guarantee that dealing with conflict will have the desired results. But God has called us to raise our children according to His righteousness. That includes conflict management. When we establish and uphold a godly standard in our home, God will do the rest.

While in college, I intended to become a high school teacher. One professor said a teacher must never let anything get past him or her in the classroom. She said, "Make your students think you have eyes in the back of your head. Respond to every situation, even if just with a stern look. If a student thinks he can get away with something, he'll never stop trying, even if he's caught." The same is true for parents. Always confront your child when conflict arises, but always do it in love. Don't say things you'll regret. Don't badger, don't malign. Never predict failure in your child, but encourage, build, and restore.

LOVE IS THE KEY

Regardless of who it's between, conflict should be dealt with in Christian love. A parent called me one day after I'd been involved in a conflict with his child. I anticipated his call and prepared a number of responses to what I thought he would say. He did call and, instead of trying to defend myself, I answered each complaint honestly and peaceably and the situation was resolved. That taught me the importance of not responding in anger. Proverbs 15:1 says, "A gentle answer turns away wrath, but a harsh word stirs up anger." That's true, whether we're dealing with our spouses, our children, or our enemies.

"The Andy Griffith Show" was one of my favorite television programs. Conflicts were always dealt with in a straightforward, loving manner. "Pa" always found out when Opie got into trouble, whether it was sassing Aunt Bea or embarrassing Barney in front of Thelma Lou. Andy and Opie talked out the problem until they found a solution, and Andy always had the end result in mind. Our conflicts aren't always as easily solved as those on "The Andy Griffith Show," but if we approach them in love, keeping our eyes on the end result, we might find them more successfully resolved.

A more reliable source of wisdom comes from the apostle Paul. He writes, "Fathers [parents], don't scold your children so much that they become discouraged and quit trying" (Colossians 3:21, TLB). And in Ephesians 6:4 he writes, "And now a word to you parents. Don't keep on scolding and nagging your children, making them angry and resentful. Rather, bring them up with the loving discipline the Lord himself approves, with suggestions and godly advice" (TLB). The importance of *lovingly* dealing with conflict can't be overstated. There's nothing less than the eternal well-being of our children at stake.

A PERFECT EXAMPLE

If we examine conflict in the life of Jesus, we have a perfect example to follow. When faced with conflict, Jesus did not *react* in anger; He *responded* in love. When faced with the adulterous woman and the hatemongers who brought her to Him, Jesus didn't beat her over the head with her sin, nor did He chastise the men for their hypocrisy. He forgave the woman, admonishing her to sin no more, and sent her would-be executioners on their way with plenty of food for thought. When Peter denied Him, Jesus didn't kick him out of the kingdom; He lovingly restored him. And, when He stood face to face with His accusers, Jesus kept silent, knowing He was about to die for these same men.

THE ULTIMATE WEAPON

As a youth pastor I inevitably become attached to the kids in my group. I share my life with them as they go through tumultuous times on their way to adulthood. Not long ago, a group of "my" kids walked away from our youth group, our church—and God. These weren't just any kids; they were leaders. One was my youth intern. They were looked up to and followed by others kids in the group. Their leaving devastated all of us.

I went through quite a time of soul-searching. Had I failed these kids? Had I not been the example I should have been? Had I been inconsistent in my walk with Christ? I considered situation after situation and wondered what I should have done differently. It was in prayer that God revealed He wanted to change hearts and lives for eternity, and He would use this conflict to do it. So, while I looked for a simple lesson on conflict resolution, God had something monumental in mind.

I realized I was acting like a defeated, pathetic youth pastor and knew it wasn't helping me, the kids in my group, or the ones who had walked away. I needed to face the enemy with the boldness of Christ and make hell tremble on their behalf; and that's just what I did, through prayer—the ultimate weapon against the powers of darkness. As a result, all but one have come back. They're stronger and have a closer relationship than ever with their heavenly Father. I'm convinced that one will also return.

God uses conflict to develop our character. "Iron sharpens iron, and one man sharpens another" (Proverbs 27:17, RSV). Our response to conflict determines the outcome. We'll either be honed and improved by it, or we'll be defeated by it. If we face it head on, and lovingly and prayerfully, we're on our way to success.

In the 1920s, Mallory led an expedition to climb Mt. Everest. The first expedition failed, as did the second. With a team of the best qualified and most able, Mallory made a third attempt. In spite of careful planning and extensive safety precautions, disaster struck. An avalanche hit, killing most of the climbers. When the survivors returned to England, a banquet was held in honor of Mallory and the others who were lost. One survivor stood to thunderous applause and looked around the hall at the framed pictures of his dead comrades. Then he turned his back to the crowd and faced a picture of Mt. Everest, which loomed a silent, unconquerable giant behind the banquet table. With tears streaming down his face, he addressed the mountain. "I speak to you, Mt. Everest, in the name of all brave men living and those yet unborn. Mt. Everest, you defeated us once; you defeated us twice; you defeated us three times. But, Mt. Everest, we shall someday defeat you, because you can't get any bigger and we can."[1] He was right.

The Reverend Kelly S. Goins graduated from Evangel College with a B. A. in Music Education, then returned to his home town of Broken Arrow, Oklahoma, where he serves as youth pastor at Broken Arrow Assembly of God. He has been involved in youth ministry for eleven years, and his youth group has grown six hundred percent since 1988. A gifted musician and songwriter, he is also a national speaker for youth camps, retreats, and revivals.

He and his wife Lisa have one daughter, Kalli.

10

The Bible, Respect, and Authority

WALT WEAVER

As a parent you've certainly earned the right to say with greater emotion than any politician, salesman, or comedian, "I get no respect!" In fact, if you were to check your dictionary for the definition of the word "father," you will find that it falls directly between "fathead" and "fatigue" in the dictionary. And "mother" falls somewhere between "motheaten" and "motion sickness." In my years of working with parents and their children, one of the most frequent complaints I hear is, "My children have no respect for me."

Each of us has been given the responsibility of teaching our children to respect God-given authority. The Bible admonishes us to "show proper respect to everyone" (1 Peter 2:17). This includes employers, teachers, pastors, and our neighbors. But this chapter will focus on *parental* respect.

RESPECT FOR PARENTS

God makes it clear we are to honor or "respect" our parents so we may live a long and prosperous life. God saw parental respect as an issue of such vital importance that He gave it to Moses as one of the Ten Commandments—second only to having no other gods and remembering or "respecting" the sabbath day and keeping it holy.

This commandment stands out as the only one God gives with the promise that if we oblige, we will live a long life. My parents firmly believed in parental respect, and, as a result, carefully engineered a plan to help me obtain longevity. This plan, at rare moments, would involve the use of an instrument known to my parents as the "spanking belt" and known to my siblings and me as the "belt of doom." I discovered on more than one occasion that Mom was quite skilled at using the dreaded belt. Some might question my parents' approach to discipline and, to be honest, there were times I didn't appreciate it. Yet, my parents had nothing less than heavenly intentions when they disciplined their children. They wanted us to learn the biblical principle that a great blessing awaits those who obey and respect the God-given authority of parental guidance.

I've heard individuals say, "I demand respect from my children!" In fact, we would be more honest if we said, "I demand *obedience* from my children!" If we demand respect from our children we rob them of the opportunity to offer it to us freely, as a gift or token of their love and devotion. Furthermore, the difference between respect and obedience is as extreme as the difference between fear and love.

For example, as punishment a father once told his disobedient son to stand in the corner. After the boy took his place, he shouted, "It may look like I'm standing, but I'm still sitting on the inside." Here is a child who obeyed his parent, but didn't respect him. Obedience can be demanded, but respect must be earned. Obedience is comparable to offering a service to an individual in which they oblige by offering you the expected amount of compensation. While, on the other hand, respect cannot be demanded any more than one could demand an individual's devotion or love.

The God-given authority we have as parents will be greatly enhanced when it is joined with God-given wisdom. James 1:5 tells us God gives wisdom generously to *anyone* who asks, without finding fault. As the farmer in the parable of the sower, we must carefully plant the seeds of respect in the hearts of our children and do everything in our power to keep these precious seeds from being choked out by actions we take as parents. All too often we follow the shallow philosophy that our children should "do what we say, not what we do." But we should be able to declare as the apostle Paul, "Whatever you have learned or received or heard from me, or seen in me—put it into practice" (Philippians 4:9). It is humbling to know with every action a parent takes, whether godly or ungodly, we declare to our children, "Whatever you have learned or seen or heard from me—put it into practice."

How can we plant seeds of respect in the heart of our children? We must start by being an example, by showing respect for those in authority over us. This includes the pagan employer whose voice sends chills down your spine; the police officer who writes you a summons for going 56 miles per hour—while others were driving much faster; the annoying neighbor who mows his grass at 7:00 a.m. on your only day off; or the spouse you may have grown to take for granted. As I have traveled the nation, I have had the privilege of conversing with many young people. In only a few moments of conversation, one can easily detect what kind of respect their parents have for others—as respect or disrespect is reflected in the voices of their children.

We can also cultivate the delicate flower of respect in our family by showing respect for our children. At times, we may find it easy to let our feelings, words, and emotions run wild when we are hidden from the eyes of our employer, friend, or church. As a result, we find it easier to treat our children as pets when they should be treated as the precious gifts they are. On the other hand, this new-age mentality—that a good parent must be a child's best friend—is almost nauseating. Our children are not in need of another friend; they need a parent. But we must make every attempt to be friendly to our children. This can be done by simply asking how their day went, what they're feeling, or what their opinion is on a subject or issue. If we ask only these questions, however, we do our families a grave injustice. We show a greater act of respect when we take the time to intently listen to their answers. May we be careful to listen to their opinions and allow them the opportunity to present their view of a situation. By listening to their opinions, we are in no way obligated to respond. Instead, we are obligated to use this information to make good, godly parental decisions.

As we examine the cultivation of respect, we must remember to take the time and respond to the so-called simple things in life—things as simple as a crayola masterpiece or dandelion bouquet. We must take the time to say things as simple as, "I love you because you are you." Or, "Thank you for a job well done." This is a simple but powerful way of cultivating both parental respect and self-respect in the lives of our children. Make certain you never require your children to read your mind when it comes to your love for them. Let them know with word and action that your love and respect for them will never fail and is never contingent upon their performance.

The difference between man and God is quite simple. A man tells his children to "get right or you'll have to leave the home!" Our heavenly Father says, "Come home and I will help you get right." How many families could have been saved if we adapted this heavenly concept? Furthermore, how many family quarrels could be avoided if a parent was honest enough to say, "I'm sorry," or perhaps a more difficult phrase, "I was wrong." Like a child using a cookie cutter to create holiday cookies, each action we make serves as a pattern for the lives of our children.

At age twelve, I set my alarm early each morning in order to have time to walk half a mile down an old gravel road to get my parents a morning newspaper. This was never something they required of me; it was something I wanted to do for them. I think in all my years, I will never forget the reward of placing the paper on the breakfast table and hearing the simple words I cherish to this day. Sometimes it was my dad and other times my mom, but someone always said, "Thank you!" As a parent may you never forget what a powerful effect one word can have in the emotional and spiritual development of a child's life. One word can fertilize or poison the delicate flower of love, confidence, or respect.

A BIBLICAL EXAMPLE

In reading the Bible, I find one parent stands out as a man who nurtured respect in the heart of his child. Abraham waited nearly one hundred years for Isaac, the son promised by God. Can you imagine the joy Abraham felt when his son was born? How he must have cherished every moment, from Isaac cutting his first tooth to hitting his first home run (or the Old Testament equivalent).

Then came the shocking day that God called Abraham to sacrifice Isaac. I find it amazing that Abraham didn't hesitate, but immediately prepared for the sacrifice. He carried the coals and the knife he would use on that long journey up the mountain while Isaac carried the wood for his own sacrifice. I've always marveled at Abraham's faith and obedience, but I'm equally amazed at Isaac's, for there is not the slightest hint that Abraham had to wrestle him to the altar. If it were me, I would have been screaming for help as I ran down the mountainside. Yet, Isaac never ran because he trusted God as well as his father.

This is a great example of one son who had faith in his father, as well as respect for God and Abraham's wisdom. Abraham had obviously proven himself in the valley; now Isaac would trust him on the mountain. Can we say the same about our children? Have we been trustworthy in the valleys of life so that our children will respect us on the mountains of decision? Isaac submitted to his father because he knew he loved him. He was faithful and he knew he was devoted to God. He had undoubtedly heard him pray many times. He had seen him live obediently before God. And he most certainly had never misled Isaac. Now, at the most crucial time of his life, Isaac respected his father enough to trust him with his life.

Abraham must have lived consistently before Isaac. Lack of consistency in our lives will stunt the spiritual growth of our children. They will never respect—or embrace—our faith if we are not consistent in faith, love, and discipline.

When Abraham told Isaac God would provide a lamb for the offering, Isaac didn't ask for proof or roll his eyes; he simply believed.

This isn't to say Abraham was a perfect father. He was human and therefore made his share of mistakes. But his walk with God was consistent, and it was reflected in the life of his son. Conversely, Isaac wasn't a perfect child. He probably got into mischief that required discipline. We can assume Abraham and Sarah were consistent in their discipline. Their consistency was as important as the type of discipline used. As parents they had to live in agreement. If they disagreed with one another in front of their son about when and how to discipline, he would not have respected their authority and would have played one parent against the other. May Abraham and Sarah serve as our example of how imperfect parents can follow God's perfect plan and as a result see faith and respect cultivated in the lives of our children.

BENDING TOWARD THE LIGHT

Proverbs 22:6 says, "Train a child in the way he should go, and when he is old he will not turn from it." The word "train" means to "bend." If we live a life that fosters respect in our children—for us and the God we serve—they'll bend toward the kingdom of God, just as a plant bends toward sunlight.

If your sons or daughters are cultivating seeds of rebellion rather than seeds of respect, go to God in prayer. Seek His wisdom. Trust His Word. Live a consistent life devoted to God, and He promises they will not turn from the "way they should go." We have God's word on it, and that word will never pass away.

The Reverend Walt Weaver is a graduate of Central Bible College and an ordained minister with the Assemblies of God. He has had nine years of full-time ministry to young people and travels as an evangelist, ministering to families across the nation and overseas. He is a featured speaker at youth camps, youth conventions, and family revivals.

He is married to his college sweetheart, Renee, and she continues to be his greatest support outside of his relationship with the Lord Jesus. His heart reaches to the youth of this nation and he knows that in order to have a powerful effect on them, he must first reach the heart of their parents.

BEHAVIOR

*Children have never been very good at listening to their elders,
but they have never failed to imitate them.*

James Baldwin

11

The Power Generation

ROB HOSKINS

The "call" to Christian parenthood is a demanding and weighty responsibility. It's a difficult task to raise our children *in* the world and yet ensure they don't become *of* the world. The call of Christ demands we raise our children to participate in the battle between the kingdom of God and the kingdoms of this world. We must enlist our children into the spiritual service of seeing their world won for Christ. When God places *His* children into our hands, we must understand He has a destiny—an eternal purpose—for them to fulfill. Just as God the Father sent His Son into the world to save it, so we, as Christian parents, bear the responsibility of teaching our children they're to be witnesses for Christ.

The challenge of raising our kids to be "good Christians" seems monumental. Raising them to be mighty spiritual warriors seems almost impossible. As the father of a strong-willed girl, I find my time and energy consumed with mundane rituals like getting her to bed on time, not letting her eat too many sweets, and making sure she picks up her toys. While trying to survive the rigors of child-rearing, my wife and I use every opportunity to instill biblical principles and a spiritual foundation in our children. We feel content knowing our kids are well-provided for and well-behaved with a good understanding of their relationship with the Lord.

The onslaught of rebellion and immorality in our present culture has placed Christian parents in a defensive posture where we constantly try to protect our children from the sins that pervade society. But we must also become *proactive* if we're to be the parents God has called us to be. God chose that kind of mother for His Son. When Mary realized her Son was to become the supreme conduit of salvation for mankind, she could have been paralyzed by fear over the tremendous responsibility placed in her hands. Instead, in Luke 1:46-55, Mary glorifies God for the position He has placed her in and, by faith, declares that all generations would call her blessed because she knows God's plan of salvation will be accomplished through her Son. We must adopt a similar attitude of spiritual optimism for our children's destiny. The task of imparting a spiritually dynamic vision in the hearts of our kids cannot be seen as a building block added after the foundation has been laid; rather we, as Mary, must recognize it to *be* the foundation. It's never been so important for Christian parents to understand this principle.

God has a season and time for all His purposes, yet His own people, Israel, didn't recognize the "fullness of time" when their Messiah was born. Good parenting demands that we know the times in which we live so we can determine what is God's perfect will for our children. The church must not be divorced from the human condition swirling around it but must merge the sociological with the spiritual to destroy the forces of wickedness and establish the message of Christ worldwide.

GLOBALIZATION

We're raising our children in the greatest season of change the world has ever seen—a time when we not only *talk* about a global village, we live in one. *Megatrends 2000* declares, ". . . a new era of globalization has begun . . . an increasingly inner connected world."[1] Free trade is the universal economic buzzword propelling us toward a global economy. Communication is developing and expanding at such a phenomenal rate that we, as John Nesbit states, ". . . have laid the foundations of an international information highway system."[2] Political walls have come tumbling down. Mikail Gorbachev, at his 1988 speech to the United Nations, declared, "The ideal of democratizing the world order has become a powerful socio-political force. The Cold War era is over, and it has given way to the age of globalization. Entertainment, arts, and sports have gone global. People everywhere now listen to the same music and watch the same television shows ("Sesame Street" is now seen in eighty-five countries of the world.)"[3] The Tuareg, the largest tribe of nomads in the Sahara, delayed their annual migration for ten days in 1983 in order to catch the last episode of "Dallas."[4] MTV is seen in almost every corner of the earth via satellite. The same music is listened to; the same books are read. We root for the same teams and cheer for universal stars. World consumerism guarantees that people eat, drink, and use the same products, creating "the world's first true world brands."[5]

Universal language. There has been a reversal of the Tower of Babel, where more and more people are speaking fewer and fewer languages. As the Director of Distribution for a worldwide ministry placing Scripture in public school systems, I'm amazed by our ever-shrinking world. Through education, the children of the world are brought together. Through research, we found that we could reach more than sixty percent of the world's children with ten languages; with twenty languages we can reach more than ninety percent. For example, Africa, which just a few decades ago was segregated by hundreds of dialects, can now be covered with only four languages.

Travel. Travel has put the world in our back yard. More than one billion passengers fly the world's airways annually. That will increase to two billion by the year 2000.[6] For about the same amount of time and money, people can now vacation on the other side of the world. I was recently in Sacramento, California, preaching a Sunday-to-Sunday missions convention. An emergency required me to be in Bratsk, Siberia, for a meeting in the middle of the week. I left on a red-eye flight Sunday night after church and arrived in time for my mid-week meeting. Then I flew to Moscow for another meeting, and arrived back in Sacramento in time for Sunday services. How small the world has become.

Food. Even food has gone global. American fast food restaurants are found in every major capital of the world, while in the United States we're eating more and more ethnic food. In the last decade, Asian restaurants grew by fifty-four percent, Mexican restaurants by forty-three percent, and Italian restaurants by twenty-six percent.[7]

LEADING THE WAY

Globalization means America is moving into the world and, like it or not, the world is coming to America. R. B. Reich states, "... as almost every factor of production—money, technology, factories and equipment—moves effortlessly across borders, the very idea of an American economy is becoming meaningless, as are the notions of an American corporation, American capital, American products and American technology."[8] Youth, always the first to change, have adapted to these global realities and are creating a global youth culture, emulating the youth culture of America. Ours is the standard for the world. How sobering to think they may be following our young people down a road of materialism, secularism, and hedonism—even though that path has left our own youth emotionally tormented, intellectually scarred, and spiritually bankrupt. Humanism combined with hedonism has taught our kids to experiment and experience more than any generation before them, yet they are the most dissatisfied generation in history. In a society where everything is right and nothing is wrong, *self* has become the guiding force. Robert Hughes, in his book, *Culture of Complaint*, writes, "The self is now the sacred cow of American culture. Self-esteem is sacrosanct, and so we labor to turn arts education into a system in which no one can fail. In the same spirit, tennis could be shorn of its elitist overtones—all you have to do is get rid of the net."[9]

With no nets, no barriers, and no rules, children grow up with no direction, no values, and no sense of morality. The results are devastating:

Violence: 135,000 children take a gun to school; every fourteen hours a child under the age of five is murdered;

homicide has replaced motor vehicle accidents as the leading cause of death below the age of one. Our murder rate is four times higher than Europe's, and our rape rate is seven times higher.[10]

Immorality: Each year there are 30,000 pregnancies among girls under the age of fifteen. The proportion of unwed teenage mothers has risen from fifteen percent to sixty-one percent since 1960. The birth and abortion rates of U. S. teens are twice those of other countries in the developed world.[11]

Despair: The teen suicide rate has quadrupled since 1950: a teenager attempts suicide every sixteen seconds.[12]

Apathy: U. S. children rank behind America's industrial competitors in school achievement tests; SAT scores have dropped for the last twenty-five consecutive years. The high school dropout rate in America is twenty-seven percent.[13]

EXPORTING IMMORALITY

I've seen firsthand the devastation in the world, influenced greatly by the American youth culture. The media has glamorized drugs and encouraged immorality and rebellion on a global scale. When I began ministering in the schools of what was the Soviet Union in 1989, I found a refreshing innocence in their young people. Separated from the "freedoms" of the Western world, they exhibited a guileless spirit, free of the immorality rampant among the youth of America. That can no longer be said. In only a few years, I've seen these same kids begin to go the way of the West: graffitied walls filled with profanity are found in their high schools; prostitution and pornography are commonplace; the spirit of greed is promoted through song, television, and video.

Through cultural imperialism, immorality has become America's greatest export. One of our teams was recently ministering in a rural community in central Russia. After the evening crusade, a seventeen-year-old girl exhibited signs of being demon possessed. Through intercessory prayer she was delivered and filled with the Holy Spirit. A team accompanied her home to pray over her house. They were shocked to find posters of American heavy metal groups hanging in her room. The demonic spirit that had possessed the girl wasn't birthed in Russia but in the United States. Columnist Georgianne Guyers writes, "Cultural imperialism infiltrates a country through radio and TV, through tourists and peacecorpmen. It walks into an ancient and tormented country such as Iran, on the cat's feet of supposedly good willed men from Sioux City, who are in reality Satan, bringing with them Big Macs, women's rights, and relativistic, intolerant values. Unlike cheeseburgers and jeans, the globalization of television is explosive and controversial because it conveys deeper values the same way that literature does. Entertainment, through the medium of languages and images, crosses over the line of superficial exchange, and enters the domain of values. It goes right to the ethos of a culture, addressing the fundamental spirit that forms its beliefs and practices."[14]

I was on an airplane headed to Moscow that stopped in Ulan Batar, Mongolia. As I sat on the plane waiting for the transit passengers to board, I wondered what the Mongolians might look like. A group of Mongolian university students on their way to study in Moscow boarded, dressed in Levi 501 jeans, heavy metal t-shirts, and listening to Walkman cassette players. Four of them sat near me and, between them, spoke seven languages. As we conversed, I discovered they admired Michael Jackson, Madonna,

Arnold Swarzennegger, and Michael Jordan, but had no idea who Jesus Christ is and had no concept of a heavenly Father or a Savior who loved them.

The powerful force of American culture has reached the shores of every nation while the message of God's Word has not.

I spent the first twelve years of my life in the Middle East, my teenage years in Western Europe, and now serve as a foreign missionary. I'm convinced the battle for the youth of our world is being fought on two fronts. If the church in America can't capture the hearts, minds, and souls of America's youth, we won't capture it in other nations of the world. But if we read the times and understand that American youth are hungry for change, we will raise up and equip the greatest army of change-agents the world has ever seen.

WHERE DO THEY GO FROM HERE?

Where does the American youth culture go from here? What do they do after trying everything their world has offered? They either rebel or give up. How do they rebel against a hedonistic, materialistic society? By becoming sel*fless* instead of sel*fish*. A desire to *give* is being birthed in a nation that was taught to keep. The "me generation" is tired of pursuing a materialistic mirage. The American family lies in ruin because pleasing *self* was paramount. The new selflessness—environmentalism, one world order, global peace—reflects a desire for harmony and love that has eluded our youth. Our worldly intentions of raising our kids to be the wealthiest, wisest, and most powerful generation in the world is self-destructive. Jeremiah 9:23,24 declares:

> Let not the wise man boast of his wisdom or the strong man boast of his strength or the rich man boast of his riches, but let him who boasts boast about this: that he understands and knows me, that I am the Lord, who exercises kindness, justice and righteousness on earth, for in these I delight . . .

True Christianity produces the kind of fruit teens of America are hungering for. In a world of inequity, hedonism, and hate, we can offer a message of justice, righteousness, and kindness. We need to raise our children to be able to convince their peers that the only true hope is found in God's redemptive plan for this world.

The hope of a new world order, free of racism, bigotry, and prejudice, is a myth. Robert Hughes, a self-professed secularist, states, "There is no new world order. Instead, we have an intractable new world disorder as all nationalist passions and religious hatreds that have been frozen emerge refreshed by their siesta."[15] The role models American youth choose to lead them out of their culture will fail them. Madonna contends she is a revolutionary against the present order of power. She says her message undermines "capitalist constructions and rejects core bourgeois thinking." This will be real news to Time Warner, which pays $60 million for the rights to her work. Some rejection![16]

The youth of America are lost children looking for true integrity and righteous role models filled with the power of the Holy Spirit. Most believe American youth are too soft and too lethargic to rebel against the culture that has failed them. Retreating from society in suicide seems to be the easiest form of escape for many. The recent craze for "grunge" music, popularized by groups like Nirvana and the Red Hot Chili Peppers, typifies the new discontentment. Called a backlash of the materialism of the 1980s, grunge encourages dressing like hobos, retreating from the mainstream, and rejecting the materialistic values of parents. But in an age of superficial rebellion, the grunge fashion became so popular it became a fashion craze from Seattle to Paris. The movement is dying because it's become part of the twisted mainstream, always looking for something new and different. But the message of grunge is clear. Alice in Chains, a popular grunge group, expresses its feelings in a song called "Dirt":

> I've never felt such frustration or lack of self-control,
> I want you to kill me and dig me under;
> I want to live no more.
> I want to taste dirty, a stinging pistol in my mouth, on my tongue;
> I want you to scrape me from the walls and go crazy like you've made me.
> You, you are so special, you have the talent to make me feel like dirt;
> You, you use your talent to dig me under and cover me with dirt.
> One who doesn't care, yeah, is one who shouldn't be;
> I've tried to hide myself from what is wrong for me.
> One who doesn't care, yeh, is one who shouldn't be;
> I've tried to hide myself from what is wrong for me.[17]

While this doesn't represent the mainstream of America's youth culture, it's an example of the growing sense of despair among teens in the United States. This despair is well-founded as the youth of America face a foreboding future. This will be the first generation of Americans who will not better their parents. Globally, noted historian Paul Kennedy, in his book, *Preparing for the 21st Century*, prophesies a bleak future for the world system.[18] Demographics do not bode well for planet Earth. By the year 2025, when our children are in their prime, the total world population will be over ten billion.[19] The brutal significance of this figure is that ninety-five percent of this growth will occur in the underdeveloped, already overpopulated southern hemisphere. The present equilibrium between the "haves" and "have-nots" will collapse. Kennedy adds, "If the developing world remains caught in its poverty trap, the more developed countries will come under siege from tens of millions of migrants and refugees eager to reside among the prosperous but aging population of the democracies. Either way, the results are likely to be painful for the richest one-sixth of the earth's population that now enjoys a disproportionate five-sixths of its wealth."[20] Kennedy ends his book, stating:

> As the cold war fades away, we face not a new world order, but a troubled and fractured planet. . . . The pace and complexity of the forces for change are enormous and daunting. If these challenges are not met, humankind will have only itself to blame for the troubles and disasters that could be lying ahead. Many earlier attempts to peer into the future concluded either in a tone of unrestrained optimism or in gloomy forebodings or in appeals for spiritual renewal.[21]

REACHING THEIR WORLD

As believers, we know what the Bible prophesies concerning this world system. It's not our place to name a day or hour for Christ's return, but it's obviously imminent. Our children, if not us, may well see firsthand the culmination of human history.

Approaching these realities from a Christian parent's perspective could cause us to react in two ways: fear could cause us to become Christian isolationists, where we try to protect ourselves and our children from the impending realities. Or we can look to God's Word and implement His kingdom principles.

Christian youth have the brightest future of any generation to come before them. They will see God's Spirit poured out on all flesh, causing the greatest revival the world has ever known. We must instill a sense of destiny in them so they won't just try to survive the future but will conquer it with a zeal for justice, righteousness, and lovingkindness. It's vital that we prepare them for what lies ahead, for Satan, our adversary, would like nothing better than to cut off the next generation from the eternal destiny and plan that God has for their lives. Herod, as a tool of Satan, hearing the Messiah was coming to change the world, attempted to slaughter every potential candidate by killing the children of Christ's generation. So it is today that Satan uses every tool, every demonic force, to try to destroy an army of young people who have a greater potential to see their world won to Christ than any generation before them. As parents, let us understand the awesome responsibility we have to make them aware of their calling, to provide an environment in which their gifts can be developed, and equip them with the tools they need to take the message of Christ's love around the world.

The Reverend Rob Hoskins, an Assemblies of God missionary, directs the Book of Life program for Life Publishers International, a ministry that distributes the Word of God in public schools around the world. He is also the founder of Affect Destiny Teams, mobilizing people in the church of America to reach their world.

Rev. Hoskins received his degree in Sociology/Anthropology from Southern California College.

He and his wife Kim have two daughters: Diandra and Natasha. They live in Pompano Beach, Florida.

12

Sex and Dating

STEVE WILSON

"Just do it. Just say no. Just wear a condom. When it comes to sex, dating, and love, the message to America's teens is confused and confusing."[1]

This was the opening sentence in a recent magazine article dealing with the teenage sex crisis in America. Even liberals are awakening to the calamity that has engulfed America's youth. The arrival of AIDS in America a decade ago was the first real warning sign that caused people to take notice. Reports informing us about the rapid increase in venereal disease, chlamydia, and herpes among teenagers soon followed. Then came the startling news that twenty percent of all AIDS patients are under thirty, and because the incubation period is eight years or more, the Center for Disease Control believes a large proportion were infected with HIV as teenagers.[2] The disease once thought to be limited to homosexuals and drug abusers was spreading on high school and college campuses. Suddenly, America was in a crisis.

In such a climate, one would think morality would be a welcome issue. Instead, this nation has avoided it at a very high cost. We've given teens information. In 1980, only three states mandated sex education; today forty-seven states formally require or recommend it, and all fifty support AIDS education. We've given them protection: condoms and other birth control devices are readily available on most campuses. What we've not given is moral instruction.

DECLINE OF MORALITY

The moral standard society once embraced has fallen victim to the sexual revolution. We live in a society that no longer has a moral code to govern actions and dictate responsible living in the area of sex. Conduct is left to individual interpretation, ethics, and personal choice. Educators, lawyers, peers, and the entertainment industry undermine the authority of parents and promote rebellion. The term "family values" has become a polarized phrase. And those who speak from this platform are considered outdated bigots who are ignorant of new truths and freedoms.

Despite all the public awareness and education, failure to address the moral issue of sex has caused this nation's sex crisis to get worse. By the time they reach twenty, three-quarters of young Americans have had sex. One-fourth of teens contract some sort of venereal disease each year. As parents and educators watch the fallout from nearly a decade of lessons geared toward disaster prevention ("Here is a diagram of the female anatomy," or "This is how you put on a condom"), there are signs this approach to learning about sex doesn't work. Teens continue to experiment with sex at an earlier age. More than one-third of fifteen-year-old boys have had sexual intercourse, as have twenty-seven percent of fifteen-year-old girls (up from nineteen percent in 1982). Among sexually active teenage girls, sixty-two percent have had multiple partners (up from thirty-eight percent in 1971).[3] The existence of gangs like the Spur Posse in Lakewood, California—where members received points for their sexual conquests—suggests that what is being taught is not being learned. We need a new approach.

Even more horrifying is that the teenage sex crisis has infiltrated the church. In many cases, those who have a moral reason to say no are not doing so. The statistics of sexual activity among Christian teenagers is alarming.

Christian parents in America have been hurled into a brutal and treacherous war. The days of ignorance regarding worldly behavior have come to an end. The battlefield is strewn with teenage victims who have abandoned their faith, morals, and convictions, choosing to listen to the voice of a liberal culture. We must wake up, for every standard we knew as teenagers is being attacked.

MEDIA INFLUENCE

Teenagers are being challenged to become sexually active by a barrage of sexual messages, themes, images, and exhortations. MTV, movies, and television are overrun with sexual innuendos. Advertisers have increasingly geared their product pitches to the minds and hearts of the youth culture. Every day the airwaves are filled with talk shows discussing—in shameless detail—acts of adultery, homosexuality, and sex changes; at night, they're crammed with shows like "Studs" and "Married with Children." Nine-hundred-number advertising appears twenty-four hours a day, using seductively-dressed women to lure viewers to make a phone call to "eliminate" loneliness.

Teenagers typically watch five hours of television each day. This means in a year they have seen nearly 14,000 sexual encounters, according to the Center for Population Options.[4] Teens also face safe sex lectures by sports heroes, graphic illustrations of sexual intercourse in the classroom, and the Calvin Klein-type ads in most magazines. "Kids are seeing a world in which everything is sensual and physical," says Dr. Richard Ratner, president of the American Society for Adolescent Psychiatry.[5] This includes the Christian teenager. There is no avoiding the battle. They are surrounded by it. Their only chance for survival is to be trained and equipped by godly parents to deal with this onslaught of filth and immorality.

PARENTAL INFLUENCE

Most teenagers desire a deeper relationship with their parents. More than clergy, school counselors, and teachers, parents have the capacity to influence the thoughts and behavior of teenagers. From the time their child begins to listen and talk, the parent is the primary voice in their life. As the years pass, new voices come into a child's life, but the parent still remains the primary influence. In the early teenage years, young people become greatly influenced by their peers, heroes, and educators. However, this new influence is not solely responsible for teenagers abandoning the principles and convictions taught by their parents. In most cases convictions are abandoned because parents no longer communicate with and affirm their teenagers. As a result, self-esteem begins to diminish, creating a vacuum in a heart that craves love, attention, and support.

A teenager's self-esteem is built by parental affirmation and by parents spending meaningful time with them. Low self-esteem is the primary reason for the sex crisis among teens. When youth begin to doubt their worth, their values decline. As a result, moral standards become low on the priority list. "If I am worthless, what good are and for what purpose do I need standards?" seems to be the dominating thought. Consequently, value is then determined by whomever gives the teenager attention. If Mom and Dad don't do it, someone else will fill the void in a teenager's life. In most cases, they will be peers and members of the opposite sex. Through attention and understanding, the teen begins to feel good, important, and valuable. An emotional bond is the result, which creates a sense of loyalty from the teen toward the one who brought value and worth into his or her life. This new allegiance to someone besides Mom and Dad can cause them to abandon previous principles and convictions. Eventually, they adopt the values of those who are now building their self-esteem. In most cases, one of the first values that is re-shaped is their attitude and outlook on becoming sexually active.

WHEN PARENTS DON'T CARE

One Friday night, having completed a speaking engagement, I pulled into a restaurant to grab a bite to eat. It was a little after midnight. After I was seated, I noticed five teenagers enter the restaurant. At first I didn't think much of it, but then I realized how late it was. These teens were no older than fifteen, yet they were without supervision. I wondered, *Where are their parents?* Curiosity got the best of me, so I went over and began to speak with them. At first they were suspicious, and we made small talk about school, sports, and things in general. Then they began to open up, and we talked for two hours. They told me things that broke my heart. These teens had just come from a concert and stopped off at the restaurant to waste some time; they were too wired to go home. When I asked about their parents, the conversation went something like this:

"Do your parents know where you are?"

"No, and they really don't care," one boy said.

"Why do you think that?"

"They never talk to me about what's going on in my life."

"They have no clue," a young girl added. "They only care about themselves and making money."

"Tell me a little about what is going on in your lives."

"Mostly bad things. I dropped out of school," another girl replied.

"Why would you drop out of school?" I asked.

"There's no reason to go. My parents don't care about my grades, so why bother?"

"If your parents were interested, would you be motivated to do better?"

"Yeah. Then I'd have some pressure on me to perform."

The conversation went from a discussion about their parents to an open forum about their sex lives. All five of these teenagers had lost their virginity by the time they were thirteen. Three of the girls had experienced abortion, one having had two abortions by the time she was fourteen. All three girls had attempted suicide at least once. One of them rolled up her sleeves and showed me the scars.

Eventually I asked why they had become sexually active. Every one said they'd been taught to wait until marriage.

However, with the diminishing role of their parents, they began to adopt the values of individuals who had given them attention.

As the discussion came to an end, I asked if I could pray with them. Afterward, as I began to walk away, one of the young men hollered, "Hey, mister!" I turned around and looked at him. With tears in his eyes he spoke the most poignant words I've ever heard. He didn't tell me I was a great person. He didn't ask for advice about his situation. No, his words echoed the emptiness in his heart left by parents who were out of touch with his needs. He said, "Thanks for caring."

I was reminded of this scene recently when I received a phone call from a desperate mother. Her voice was panicky as she told me that she and her daughter needed to meet with me right away. Fifteen minutes later they arrived at my office. The mom walked in with red eyes, smeared make-up, and a look of hopelessness. The girl looked much older than she was, and it was obvious that my office was the last place on earth she wanted to be. Her mother began to explain the story to me. Her daughter was only thirteen, but she no longer listened to her. She came home when she wanted, had a twenty-one-year-old boyfriend, and had been pregnant twice. "I no longer have any control," the mother cried. "What can I do to get my child's love back?" After a few questions I discovered the mother had been disinterested in her daughter's life for the past three years. As a result, her daughter had done as she pleased. When there was a problem, Mom didn't have time to deal with it, so "Christy" found answers elsewhere. She abandoned the teachings of her childhood because Mom was too busy to talk, give advice, or steer her child down the right path. She was too busy to care.

COMMUNICATION: KEY TO SUCCESS

To keep our Christian teenagers on the straight and narrow in these turbulent times, parents must care enough to keep the communication channels open. This is not the time to be too embarrassed to speak to them about their sex and dating lives. Ignoring the issue will almost guarantee that a teenager will lose his or her virginity and become sexually active. Christian parents must realize it is not the church or school's responsibility to educate our children about sex and dating. It's a *parent's* responsibility, and they must care enough to speak out.

Dating and sex are topics that consume the thoughts of teenagers. They are two issues teens are confronted with daily. Our culture will not let them forget about these issues and neither will their peers. With so many "sex-crazed" voices screaming at the hearts and minds of youth today, it's vitally important they have deeply embedded guidelines and truths. Parents have the best platform to speak from, yet, in many cases, they have abdicated their authority in this area, refusing to instruct their teenagers on this topic. I believe this is the main reason for the sex crisis that is infecting our culture and our churches.

Regrettably, parents are under the misconception they have nothing of value to say. Traditionally, it has been the role of parents to convey the messages about love and intimacy. Although today's parents are veterans of the "free love" era, that doesn't make them any more able to talk about sex with their children. And it doesn't help that parents are portrayed by the entertainment industry as outdated and unknowledgeable, and that everything they say is from the "old school" and not applicable in today's society. Parents must reject this lie if they expect their kids to. You're the primary voice in the life of your teenager. Generally, teens won't communicate this, but it's true. And despite what the entertainment industry would like you to think, you still have God-given authority over your children. This doesn't mean they will heed or respect everything you say, but values will be embedded in their hearts that they can rely on in times of decision making, as long as you continue to speak into the lives of your children.

TAKE THE LEAD

How can this be accomplished? First, parents must pursue an open relationship of communication and address these topics of discussion. In most cases, teenagers won't. Statistics tell us that teen/parent relationships wane as the teen grows older.[6] Usually this is due to a lack of interest on the parent's part. Deep inside, teens desire and need a healthy relationship with their parents, but in most cases they won't pursue it. Here are some ways we can communicate with our teens on these issues:

Be on their side. Teens often feel their parents are the enemy. They cover up their actions, hide their feelings, and avoid sharing problems and struggles with their parents because they fear they'll be reprimanded. We need to create an environment where teens will talk openly about every area of their life, including dating. This kind of environment must be developed over a period of time. If we practice good communication skills early, it should be easy to maintain during the teen years. But, remember, it's never too late to start.

Give them freedom to fail. When they fail, affirm them. Show them why they failed, but do it in a positive manner.

Many parents come down hard on their teenagers in times of failure. This does nothing but push the teenager into a shell of isolation. On the other hand, by being positive in moments of failure, we establish trust within the relationship.

Discuss the struggles we faced while growing up. We should still be able to recall the insecurities, temptations, hassles, and frustrations we faced as teenagers. If we share them with our kids, they'll know we truly understand how they feel. We should talk about what dating was like for us when we were their age. Some kids will find it humorous; others will be embarrassed. Nonetheless, it will help us build an environment where our teens feel free to talk about sensitive issues.

Allow teens to make their own decisions. Often I see parents give advice and then make decisions for their teens. This pushes young people away from their parents. The perception is: Mom and Dad don't trust me to make my own decisions; therefore, I'll no longer share intimate feelings with them. Eventually they close up to their parents.

When we disagree with them or restrict them from certain activities, tell them why. In his book, *Ten Mistakes Parents Make With Teenagers,* Jay Kesler writes, "Young people need to hear a clear *why* behind the *don't.*"[7] Answering the "why" questions involves sitting down and reasoning through the consequences of certain actions and activities. As parents we must *educate,* not *indoctrinate.*

Start discussions about sex and dating early. Children learn about sex today on the elementary campus. This generation is growing up faster than any before it. An environment should be created for them to openly discuss these issues, but it will only happen if *we* take the initiative. If you have older teenagers, start talking about the subject now. Start by asking them to share what their schools teach about sex. Get their feelings about the culture and the sexual practices of teenagers today. Remember, we're trying to create an environment of open expression and communication, so we can remain a major influence in their lives.

When our teenagers recognize we're on their side, we'll be able to communicate principles and encourage biblical standards in the areas of dating and sex.

DATING

Perhaps the greatest problems facing Christian teens today fall in the category of dating and "love" relationships. Nothing has more of an emotional pull on the life of a teenager. Young people are consumed with love and dating, though they are often confused by the subject. Today's teens are bombarded with voices, giving them advice along with a false impression of love. Because many of the voices contradict one another, teens find themselves in a state of confusion.

Teenagers experience frustration, disappointment, and depression in their dating lives for myriad reasons: sexual temptation, low self-esteem, negative experiences, peer pressure, and false expectations. I've counseled with teenagers on this subject more than any other and found they are looking for answers and advice.

In his book, *Dating: Guidelines from the Bible*, Scott Kirby gives an excellent definition of dating: "When we talk about dating, we are not so much talking about a date as we are about a relationship between a guy and a girl. Dating can be better understood if it is looked at in the context of all opposite-sex relationships. There are four levels of opposite-sex relationships; each level based upon the level beneath it and vitally dependent on success in the lower level. The better one succeeds in the lower levels, the better he will succeed in the next level."[8] Kirby describes these four levels as follows:

> The first and primary relationship is *friendship*. The better one is at developing good friendships, the better chances he has for success in dating relationships. If you get your teen to begin preparing themselves for good dating relationships, then you need to help them focus on developing good friendships. It is vital that you communicate this to them. The second level of opposite-sex relationships is *dating*. There are three kinds of dates: casual, special and steady. After dating comes engagement. *Engagement* is the third level of opposite-sex relationships. Following engagement is *marriage*, which is the final level of opposite-sex relationships.[9]

In discussing the subject of dating with our teenagers, communicate that dating is establishing opposite-sex relationships. Give reasons why they should date. Let them know it's much more than having someone to "make out" with or someone to make them look good. Kirby presented several sound reasons for dating:[10]

To grow socially, emotionally, and spiritually. Dating is a way in which teenagers learn to enhance and sharpen their social skills. They also develop a better understanding and appreciation for others who are different. In his book, *Givers, Takers and Other Kinds of Lovers,* Josh McDowell shares some insight in this area. "As a teen matures, their skills in interpersonal relationships, conversation, and understanding need to grow up with them. Dating is a terrific way for a teen to learn more about themselves, to become skilled at sensing the needs and feelings of another person, and to learn how to turn that insight into responsive action."[11]

Spiritual growth can also take place during the dating years. Christian teens who trust God to bring friends of the opposite sex into their lives, and then obey God's commands within the relationship, will experience God's best for their lives. But the opposite also holds true. Kirby states, "A dating relationship helps a teenager grow either toward God or away from God."[12] In my years of youth ministry, I have seen dating relationships make a positive influence on teenage lives. Tragically, I've also seen relationships draw young people away from God. When I think back on some of the negative experiences, many of the young people involved in those relationships didn't understand the purpose of dating and the benefits dating could bring. It truly can be a pleasant and maturing time in the life of a teenager.

To learn how to better communicate with the opposite sex. Many marriages today fail because of poor communication skills. Communication is a subject no one seems to teach, but every one needs to learn. Most teenagers communicate on a superficial level, and that soon becomes boring. They look for other ways to express themselves, and that often leads to a physical relationship. Teaching teens to communicate with the opposite sex is an important task for parents today. They need to understand that communication involves *listening* as well as *speaking,* and that communication can also be non-verbal. We can help save our teens from the heartache of broken relationships by teaching them good communication skills.

To help fulfill the need to love and to be loved. Through relations with the opposite sex, teenagers learn how to cultivate attitudes and actions of unconditional love. Through the dating experience, teens develop an understanding of what it means and feels to love and be loved in a romantic way. We should explain the meaning of love, using 1 Corinthians 13 as a guideline, and encourage our teens to express and demonstrate these actions within their dating relationships.

To have a good time and relax. Teenagers face tremendous pressures today. With broken family relationships, racial tension, peer pressure, and insecurities, teens are being forced to grow up faster than any previous generation in America. Young people need positive, recreational diversions. Dating provides opportunities to get away from the hassles and problems they face. It allows them to have a good time with someone they care about while learning how to be comfortable with members of the opposite sex. Dating should be fun and rewarding, free of pressure. Parents who emphasize that will help take the pressure off the dating experience.

To help shape an ideal image of their future mate. Dating allows teenagers to develop ideas about the qualities they'd like to see in a future mate. Through dating they're made aware of personality traits they may or may not find attractive, and they discover what is truly important in a relationship. We can help our teens know what qualities to look for, reminding them they will eventually marry someone they've dated.

CHRISTIANS DATING NON-CHRISTIANS

This subject is the most controversial one we'll discuss with our teenagers, especially if they've already started dating. We must not be afraid to address it and must not accept the excuses and rationalizations our teens may offer. We must stand firm and not compromise. The Bible is very clear on this issue. "Do not be yoked together with unbelievers. For what do righteousness and wickedness have in common? Or what fellowship can light have with darkness? What harmony is there between Christ and Belial? What does a believer have in common with an unbeliever?" (2 Corinthians 6:14,15).

I've never seen anything positive come from a Christian/non-Christian relationship, whether in dating or marriage. In fact, I've only seen tragedy. I often hear teens declare, "I'm going to lead him or her to the Lord. This is the only way I can influence him or her for God." I tell them, "The only leading in that relationship will be done by the unbeliever. Before you lead them to the Lord, they'll lead you to bed."

God will not bless blatant disobedience. The Spirit of the Lord does not move in that type of environment. If there happens to be a conversion, in most cases it won't last. As soon as a break-up occurs, the unbeliever returns to his old ways, having never really committed himself to Christ out of hatred for his sin and recognizing his need for God. Probably the "commitment" was made out of pressure to please the person the unbeliever was dating.

Teens will say, "I'm not planning to marry the person. ... I just want to date them." As my friend Rich Wilkerson would say, "Famous last words!" In his book, *Teenagers, Parental Guidance Suggested,* Wilkerson suggests you "ask the woman who is married to an unbeliever; have her describe to you the agonies she has endured, the bitter pain, the disappointment, unfaithfulness, drinking and involvement in a lifestyle that is entirely out of step with this girl's upbringing and Christian beliefs. And oh, how about all the wasted years."[13] If a person *dates* an unbeliever, they will consider *marrying* one. Once a person gets emotionally and romantically involved, it's much harder to end a relationship. Eventually the Christian will lose spiritual discernment, followed by a rapid decay of his or her spiritual life. Then their heart will become cold toward spiritual things, and they'll lose their desire to pursue the ways of God.

Let us wake up. We cannot neglect this of all issues. Our kids need to understand dating non-Christians will bring pain, disappointment, heartache, and perhaps spiritual death.

REAL BEAUTY LIES WITHIN

We're a society that judges people by their external features. Hollywood has been selling this message to teenagers for years, and so successfully that teenagers are having plastic surgery because they're unhappy with their appearance. Young people are taught to look at the outward appearance in deciding who to go out with. Ours is a very superficial world.

Emphasizing the external rather than the internal is diametrically opposed to what God emphasizes, for He is far more concerned with inward character than outward appearance. The real beauty of a person lies in who they are, not what they look like. The adage "beauty is only skin deep" may be old, but it's not obsolete. We need to teach our teenagers the importance of looking beyond the physical, sharing the importance of seeking inner qualities such as positive values, attitudes, goals, personality, likes and dislikes. We should emphasize the need to ask God for wisdom and discernment in their dating life. God will never let them down if they include Him in the dating process.

LOOKING FOR MR. OR MS. RIGHT

Teens must realize it's more important to *be* the right person than to *find* the right person. Many young people spend more time looking for Mr./Ms. Right than developing their own character. They need to focus on conforming more and more to the image of God. When their lives are correctly prioritized God will bring that special person into their life; they won't need to search. We should share this truth with our teenagers and remind them of it often. It will eliminate some of the pressure and help them overcome their insecurities.

SEX

The sexual revolution in America has created a physical, moral, and social crisis. The following truths may keep our teenagers from becoming a victim of the fallout:

God is not opposed to sex. Many Christians feel that pleasurable sex is carnal and therefore sinful. Nothing could be further from the truth. God created sex, complete with all its excitement and passion. He could have allowed us to reproduce like fish, animals, or plants; He could have made it a mundane experience. But He didn't. He made it to be enjoyed within the confines of marriage.

If teens are to have a healthy attitude about sex—and consequently a satisfying marriage relationship—we need to teach them about it openly and honestly. Ignoring the subject sends the message that sex is taboo, rather than something that God created for our pleasure.

Sex outside of marriage is wrong. Christian teenagers know that sex outside of marriage is wrong, but in many cases they don't know why. They understand that God says it's wrong, but they don't fully understand His reasons. Here are some reasons you can share with your teenager on why they should wait.

Sexual involvement outside of marriage brings guilt rather than fulfillment. After petting or intercourse, many teens feel dirty, used, and guilty. "It wasn't what I expected it to be," they say. And they're right; it wasn't—for a very good reason. It lacked intimacy. A couple must have commitment if they want to enjoy intimacy, and sex without intimacy is disappointing. Intimacy involves emotional union as well as physical. Generally speaking, teenage boys who engage in sex do so for physical gratification, while teenage girls usually do so for emotional gratification. Both will be unfulfilled because they violate the principles that God built into the sexual experience. The following is a perfect illustration:

> I had been told all my life that sex before marriage was wrong, but no one ever told me why. In the twelfth grade, I found myself dating one boy for a long period of time. We spent a lot of time alone and as a result, our relationship became more physical. I felt guilty, bitter, frustrated and dirty. I would say to him, "We need to stop having sex, or at least slow down." Well, we tried to slow down,

but that didn't work. Instead of getting closer, we grew further apart. After two years of dating I finally said, "No more sex," and he said "goodbye." Since then, whenever I dated another person for a length of time, sex became a part of the relationship. Tears always came because I had blown it again.[14]

Tragic. Yet this story is the same for thousands of teenagers.

There's only one first time. Sex outside of marriage is not wrong because it's naughty. It's wrong because it gets in the way of something better.[15] That first sexual experience should be memorable. It should be with your life-partner. Josh McDowell shares some excellent insight: "What a joy it is to be able to share that first time with the one committed to you for life! God's provision for marriage is that first time bond, the memory of an act of love that made the relationship complete. Even if the wedding night is awkward, rushed, or maybe a little painful, the memory of having first made love with one's life-long partner often overrides all that."[16]

Sexually transmitted diseases. We've reached the point in our culture when sex can be a death sentence. How ironic: the act God created to bring joy, happiness, and fulfillment now kills. God never intended this to happen. But violating His laws brings consequences. Many young people have the attitude "it will never happen to me," but that's a false assumption. Over twelve million new cases of sexually transmitted diseases occur in America each year. At this rate, one in four Americans between the ages of fifteen and fifty-five will eventually acquire a sexually transmitted disease (STD). Teenagers must be warned. We might ask them, "If everyone waited until marriage to have sex and then remained faithful to their partners, would there be any sexual diseases?" God tells us to wait for a reason. He loves us and wants to protect us from a life of pain and suffering.

More reasons to wait include loss of virginity, unwanted pregnancy, forced marriage, painful memories and flashbacks, self-hatred, illegitimate children, and damaged family relationships. The list is endless.

THE BIG LIE

The media ranks third in its power to influence youth. Only parents and peers have a more powerful effect on teenagers. Understanding this, it's important for parents to expose the lies and misconceptions promoted by the media. From soap operas to movies, Hollywood presents sex outside of marriage as fulfilling, natural, and rewarding—a casual act that has nothing to do with lovemaking. They neglect to portray characters who acquire sexually transmitted diseases, who are faced with unwanted pregnancy, whose lives are ruined. No one pays the price for illicit sex in Hollywood. This sends a strong message to teenagers, giving them the impression that everything will end happily if they become sexually active. Even commercials promote the lie. If you drink a certain type of beer, beautiful women will follow you and desire your attention. If you drive a certain type of vehicle, you'll attract beautiful women. Our youth are bombarded with these types of messages. The media has misrepresented casual sex and free love, leaving youth with dreams and fantasies about sex that could never be fulfilled.

We must destroy the myth and expose the lie. God created sex as an intimate act between husband and wife

Sex and Dating

that causes them to be "one flesh." The benefits of waiting for marriage and remaining faithful after marriage will bring the joy that God intended. It will be one of the most important conversations we have with our teenagers.

STARTING OVER

More than likely there are parents reading this chapter whose teenagers have already experimented with sex. You're upset and heartbroken and wonder how you should address this issue. Consider these words of advice:

Love them unconditionally. Hate the act, but love the person. Be sensitive to their failure and help them through the difficulties they'll face because of their actions. Don't be judgmental. Remember, God restores us when we fail. He may use you as the instrument of restoration.

Forgive them. Let them hear from your lips, "I forgive you." This will help relieve the pain and guilt your young person is experiencing. It will also affirm that God forgives.

Pray with them. Parents are often quick to judge but slow to pray with their teens. Remember, when we confess our failures and commit our lives to God, the Holy Spirit can take control of the situation and turn a negative situation into something positive. And it's not enough to pray *for* them; pray *with* them. The rewards will be eternal.

Assure them of God's cleansing power. Share examples from the Bible of those who failed in this area but were given another chance. Since God is no respecter of persons, the same forgiveness is available to them. While they can never regain their physical virginity, they can regain their spiritual and emotional virginity. Through the process of confession and accepting God's forgiveness, your teen is pure and chaste in the eyes of God.

By instructing our teenagers in the area of sex and dating, they will develop healthy dating habits, a positive outlook and understanding of sex, and stand a far better chance of having the successful, fulfilling marriage God intended.

The Reverend Steve Wilson is president of ChurchCare International—a ministry committed to helping needy churches in the unreached parts of the world. He and his wife Robin have flown more than a million miles bringing the gospel to remote areas around the globe. Steve has coordinated hundreds of missions trips for churches, Bible colleges, and other ministry groups.

He is a graduate of Bethany College and has ten years of youth ministry experience.

13
Understanding Teenagers

DONNY BURLESON

In Sacramento, California, there's a public service announcement that comes on television every evening. The background is of an inner city park with the camera focused on an empty swing set with one swing gently moving back and forth. A concerned voice says, "It's ten o'clock. Do you know where your kids are?"

For several decades, teachers have been asked to identify the top problems facing America's high school classrooms. In 1940, teachers identified talking out of turn, chewing gum, making noise, running in the halls, cutting in line, dress code infractions, and littering as major problems plaguing schools. Tragically, these "behavior problems" have been replaced with drug and alcohol abuse, pregnancy, suicide, rape, robbery, and assault. Perhaps an appropriate public service announcement could be aired all across the nation, saying, "America, it's the 1990s. Do you know where your kids are?"

John 21:1-17 relates the account of Jesus showing Himself to His disciples after He had risen from the dead. He stepped on the scene to find His disciples in a desperate situation, much like today's generation of young people. The disciples had been in a boat fishing all night but had caught nothing. Why were they fishing? The answer is simple: they had been fishermen before Christ came into their lives; now that He was gone, they had returned to their old ways. They were in that boat because the bottom had dropped out of their world.

Peter, for example, was there because all he'd believed in had failed him. He had given up everything, including his father and business, to follow Jesus. He had committed everything to the cause of Christ. Then, without warning, the bottom dropped out. Jesus was arrested, convicted, and put to death as a criminal. No one, including Peter, understood that Jesus had to die to fulfill God's plan for fallen man. Dejected and angry, he believed Christ had let him down. It was then—while the disciples wallowed in doubt and defeat—that Jesus walked back into their lives.

HOPELESS

If Jesus were to walk on the shores of America, He'd find a *hopeless* generation, much like He found in the boat that morning; hopeless because the moral fibers of our nation have been stripped away. Many of today's teens have grown up without moral instruction. There are no absolutes. No right and wrong, no black and white, only shades of gray. Everything is debatable; nothing concrete. We live in an era when people are more concerned about "rights" than truth.

The Statue of Liberty stands proudly in the New York Harbor, a symbol of freedom. Yet, when one walks the streets of New York, every type of corruption and depravity is in sight. It won't take long to ask, "Is this what freedom has brought us?"

"Family" has become the "F" word of the 1990s. A word that should bring feelings of love, warmth, and stability today produces feelings of hurt, anger, and insecurity. An assemblyman who served on a national committee for the needs of the American family said it took more than a year to agree on a definition of "family." It's no wonder hopelessness has gripped our youth. With the divorce rate soaring above fifty percent, this generation has introduced new terms such as "single parent," "broken home," and "dysfunctional family."

Our priorities have been misplaced, and our kids are the losers. For example, more importance is placed on having a nice house and driving a nice car than on spending quality time with the family. An advertisement produced by Tony Campolo Ministries shows a Mercedes Benz and a child with the caption, "Who switched the price tags?" Nearly eighty-five percent of teens say they don't feel loved. When we examine America's priorities, such a statistic isn't surprising.

HELPLESS

If Jesus were to walk the shores of America, He'd also find a *helpless* generation. All we offer for the problems of our young people today is a list of alternatives. This generation experiences an epidemic drug problem, and we offer clean needles. Premarital sex is out of control, producing an escalation in the number of teen pregnancies and sexually transmitted diseases, and we offer condoms. Alcohol abuse was reported by the Gallup poll in 1990 to be the number one threat to teens, resulting in 4.5 million teenage alcoholics,[1] and we offer a ride home when they're drunk. It's like building a hospital at the bottom of a cliff because kids are going over the edge. Our actions say, "We don't know how to keep you from life's pitfalls, so we'll patch you up when you do fall." That isn't good enough. Our young people don't need alternatives, they need answers. The gospel of Christ provides them. To a world that was lost, Jesus said, "I am the way." To a world that was confused, He said, "I am the truth." To a world that was dying, He said, "I am the life" (John 14:6). Jesus is the answer for every problem we face today.

OUT OF CONTROL

If Jesus were to walk the shores of America, He would find a generation *out of control*. In the 1960s, we lost our innocence; in the 1970s, we lost our morals; in the 1980s, we lost our hope. Now we have nothing left to lose. Perhaps the intensified rebellion we see in our youth is due to a tenuous, uncertain future. They've been disappointed by parents, politicians, and preachers, and an unprecedented recklessness is the result. The philosophy of ". . . eat, drink, and be merry . . ." (Ecclesiastes 8:15, NKJV) seems to characterize this generation.

William J. Bennett, co-director of the Heritage Foundation, reports a 560 percent increase in violent crime in the past thirty years. The illegitimate birth rate has increased by more than 400 percent, the divorce rate has quadrupled, and the percentage of children living in single-parent homes has tripled. Sadly, but not surprising, the teen suicide rate has increased 200 percent.

These statistics reflect a fire that rages out of control in this generation, a fire directly connected to our future. And, as Mario Marillo states, "Fire never says, 'That's enough!'"

Many are in denial of the devastation sweeping America. They attach labels such as "freedom of choice" or "freedom of expression" and close their eyes to the damage. We're in a national state of emergency, but no one admits it until their own children become statistics. The AIDS epidemic is a perfect example: it doesn't hit home until we know someone with AIDS, and according to the Surgeon General, by 1995 everyone in the world will. Then it will be real to us. We must not wait for the fire to reach our doorstep before we respond. What can be done to extinguish it before it destroys our future? First, we must have an understanding of the problem.

Young people face tremendous pressure today—from peers and the media—to drink alcohol, use drugs, join gangs, and practice illicit sex. We have to give them a reason to say no. I once participated in a debate on the subject of providing birth control to teens on campus. Other groups, such as Planned Parenthood, had also been invited to share their views on the issue. As I shared the biblical perspective on sex before marriage, I was met with disbelief and opposition. Only then could I truly empathize with Christian youth who face such opposition daily. They must feel overwhelmed at times as they swim against the current. The pressure to conform beats at them relentlessly and can weaken their resolve unless we're there to strengthen and encourage.

CRY FROM WITHIN

Drug and alcohol abuse, gang participation, and illicit sex are not the problems of America's teenagers; they're the answers. One Wednesday night, on my way to a youth service, I stopped at McDonald's. While sitting at the drive-thru waiting to order, I was startled as an automobile came to a screeching halt on the street just a few feet from me. A huge, burly character jumped out of his car, slammed the door, threw down his soda, and began shouting obscenities as he yanked open the passenger door and flipped the seat forward. He reached into the back seat, grabbed a sixteen-year-old girl by the shirt, pulled her out of the car, and began to beat her as he held her against the car. I got out of my car and tried to calm the young man down. He ignored me but suddenly jumped back into his car and drove away, leaving the girl behind. With her shirt ripped, she walked away in tears. I ran to catch up with her to see if I could help. Meanwhile, a passing sheriff was summoned. I assured him the girl was okay, and when he left to pursue the assailant, I asked the young girl if I could take her home. Since our youth service was about to start, I drove to the church, gave her a youth group t-shirt, and had two girls in the group take her home. A couple weeks later, a girl from our church recognized the shirt and invited her to a youth service. That night she invited Jesus into her heart.

We could be critical and say she got what she deserved for being with a guy like that. But she wasn't looking for someone to abuse her. She was looking for someone to love her. I could almost hear her cry: "Will somebody please love me . . . tell me I'm valuable . . . accept me? I want to be important, and if all I have to do is drink with you, take drugs with you, or sleep with you, that's a small price. Just tell me you love me." Drugs, alcohol, and sex aren't the problem—they're the symptom. But too many young people think they're the answer to the need they have to be accepted. If we'll only listen, we'll hear their silent cry:

"I don't want to be with him, but I hate to be alone."

"My mom's an alcoholic. Tonight she was so drunk I had to help her get undressed."

"I'm scared . . . and I'm tired of the hangovers and coming down. I'm tired of running from everything."

"I got involved with a guy who said he loved me. When I got pregnant, he left."

"My father raped me. I loved him. Why would he hurt me?"

"I tried to overdose because my parents keep telling me how worthless I am."

These real accounts are from Dawson McAllister's, *Please Don't Tell My Parents*.[2] We have to open our ears to the cry of this generation. At twelve years of age, my step-dad walked out of my life. He was my hero, my everything. His leaving broke my heart. He left after a fight with my mom. Fights were nothing new around my house; neither was my dad's leaving. But this time I knew it was for good. I watched as he went through the house and gathered things he wanted to take with him. I followed as he went outside to put his tools in his truck. I somehow knew I'd never see him again, and I went into the house and wept. When he came back to say a final goodbye, he said, "Son, it's not your fault. Your mother and I just can't get along anymore." But it didn't matter what he said. All I knew was that I wasn't important enough for him to stick around.

I tried to silence the cry of my heart, like so many kids today. I tried drugs, alcohol, and one relationship after another—anything that would make me feel valuable. But nothing eased the pain until Jesus came into my life.

COMFORT

Jesus found His disciples tired and discouraged after fishing all night in vain. The words He spoke are relevant for our young people who have looked everywhere without satisfying the ache in their hearts. First, He *comforted* them.

He called to His disciples and said, "Come and eat." In that culture, sharing a meal with someone was the highest form of fellowship. You can almost hear Him say, "Hey fellows! It's going to be all right. Come on back to shore. I know how you feel. I know the hurt and uncertainty. I know the feelings of hopelessness and the sense of failure you're going through. Come and eat. Nothing has changed. I still love you."

This generation of youth has been racked with pain and heartache like never before. Broken homes and shattered dreams have left them empty and hurting. They've been abandoned and disappointed. They're asking, "Is anything true? Is there anything I can depend on; anyone I can trust?"

One of my fellow workers met a twelve-year-old boy in the apartment complex where he lived. He told the boy he was a youth pastor and asked if he'd like to come to church with him. The boy responded with an enthusiastic yes. My friend told him he'd pick him up at 8:00 a.m. on Sunday, but the boy said, "You won't come." Again, my friend said he would be there at 8:00 a.m., but the boy repeated, "You won't come. No one ever comes." A few months later we learned why the boy was so doubtful. He'd been waiting for his dad to call since he was three years old. Every year he'd say, "My Dad is going to call me this year." He always hoped; he always waited; but the call never came.

The gospel provides comfort for the hurting heart. The Bible says God is a Father to the fatherless, that He binds up broken hearts and sets at liberty those who are bruised. The message Jesus has for this hurting generation of youth is a word of comfort. He says to them as He did His disciples, "Come and eat."

CONFRONT

Second, Jesus *confronted*. This generation is not only a hurting generation, it's a rebellious one. Second Timothy so accurately describes these troubled times that it's like reading any local newspaper in America:

> But mark this: There will be terrible times in the last days. People will be lovers of themselves, lovers of money, boastful, proud, abusive, disobedient to their parents, ungrateful, unholy, without love, unforgiving, slanderous, without self-control, brutal, not lovers of the good, treacherous, rash, conceited, lovers of pleasure rather than lovers of God—having a form of godliness but denying its power. Have nothing to do with them—2 Timothy 3:1-5.

To this generation, Jesus says, "Repent!"

The balance of comfort and confrontation is important. We understand that pain is a major cause for the rebellion. But it's not an excuse. When bitten by a snake, you can get mad and call the snake a snake. You can curse it, step on it, or even kill it. But at some point you'd better get the poison out or it will kill you.

COMMISSION

Third, Jesus *commissioned*. God has a purpose for the wayward youth of this generation. After Jesus comforted and confronted Peter, He instructed him to "feed my lambs." Those words would compel him for the rest of his life. They were like food and water to a dying man. God has the same word for kids today who are dying of boredom and lack of purpose. He says, "I have a plan and a purpose for your life. I want to use you in a mighty way."

Jeremiah 29:11 says, "For I know the thoughts that I think toward you, says the Lord, thoughts of peace and not of evil, to give you a future and a hope" (NKJV). I was going nowhere and doing nothing with my life until I met Jesus. Now my life is incredible, and I'm excited about the plan God has for me. God wants to do the same in each and every person He's created. Jesus Christ can make it happen. We must expose our young people to the One who comforts, confronts, and commissions.

Donny Burleson has been working with teenagers for over ten years. He spent two years at Bethel Church of San Jose under Pastor Charles Crabtree and seven years at Capital Christian Center with Pastor Glen Cole. He is a man who understands the needs of this generation. He and his wife, Jamie, and their two daughters, Kayla and Kortney, travel full-time as evangelists and make their home in Sacramento, California.

14

Clothes, Hair, and Makeup

RANDY GREER

For ten years I was deeply involved in ministry to teenagers, and I found it relatively easy to counsel parents on decisions involving their children. Then a teenager invaded *our* home. Our oldest daughter Brandie hit the adolescent stage and the real challenge began. Now I know why experts say raising kids is like taking a canoe ride, and the teen years are the white-water rapids. Each day presents new challenges with decisions that must be made quickly in uncharted territory.

Parents have no reason to dread these years; potentially they can be the most rewarding of the parent-child relationship. God's Word provides necessary guidelines to help us make wise decisions and "make the most of every opportunity" (Colossians 4:5).

WHAT'S ON THE MENU?

To properly discuss clothes, hair, and makeup, we must first take a look at what motivates style choices. In other words, this chapter is supposed to be about french fries, but first let's take a close look at the hamburger. One of my favorite scriptural principles, pointed out in a sermon by Dr. George O. Wood, is that "God is more concerned with what's happening *in* me than what's happening *to* me." (See 1 Samuel 16:7.) Most of the time, our clothing, hair, and makeup are a reflection of what's happening deep inside us.

Wise parents will help their teens work on inner character and beauty instead of concentrating on the outward appearance. It's best to begin when our kids are young, before their cement has had a chance to dry, but there's no time like the present to make a new beginning.

BACK TO THE BASICS

In his book, *Growing Wise in Family Life,* Chuck Swindoll points out four biblical truths from Deuteronomy 6 that are a must for any healthy family. I suggest you turn there and circle the four words that represent these truths: *Hear* (vs.4), *Love* (vs.5), *Teach* (vs.7), *Fear* (vs.13).[1]

Hear the truth continually. Moses thought it was most important for his fellow Israelites to understand the foundation of their faith: Jehovah is unique, unlike any other deity; He is unity, One in essence, One in harmony; He alone is God. This knowledge brought a sense of security to the Israelites. The gods of their polytheistic neighbors were unpredictable: just because you were loyal to one didn't mean you were protected from another; but Jehovah is ever-faithful.

The God we serve is eternally existent in three Persons, who have revealed to us a righteous standard that is consistent, immovable, unshakable. "Hear, O Israel: The

Lord our God, the Lord is one" (Deuteronomy 6:4). Or, as Swindoll paraphrases, our children need to consistently *hear* "the Lord is our God. We acknowledge His presence, His uniqueness, His place, His right to rule over us. We seek His will, we endeavor to walk in His way."[2] The family that *hears* the truth continually will live in harmony.

Strong families lean on these incredible truths from the Word of God. When times get tough and the future becomes uncertain, we must reaffirm our confidence in God and determine to trust Him, no matter what. We must consistently let it be known in our homes that the Lord is our God. He can be trusted without reservation. His will is perfect. All that happens to us fits beautifully into the plan He has for our lives.

I remember speaking for a youth camp in the fall of 1980. I had just finished my third season as an outfielder with the Philadelphia Phillies and was earnestly praying about making a transition into the local church to work with young people. At that time, Lipton tea commercials were showing people falling refreshingly into a pool of water. I decided to illustrate trust to my group of kids by selecting a young man to come up and, with eyes closed, fall back into my arms. I'd know that he truly trusted me if he could keep his feet together as he fell. It worked so well that I decided to blindfold him and stand him up on a chair. I wanted the effect to be breathtaking, so I thought I'd catch him just before he hit the ground. I caught him—but not before he bounced off the floor twice! Though it's difficult to trust man, our children need to know God can be trusted. He is consistent, He is faithful, He is always there.

We should stop and think about what's being heard in our homes. Do the television programs we watch, the videos we rent, and the music we listen to carry a message consistent with what we teach and believe? If so, we'll raise secure kids who will not be easily swayed by every new fashion statement that comes along. Their security will not rely solely on dressing and wearing their hair and makeup like everyone else because what they've heard through the years has contributed to the building of their faith. (See Romans 10:17.) Their security comes from their relationship with God. Peer pressure these days is enormous—worse than anything we were ever subjected to; but kids who have *heard* kind and encouraging words, as opposed to bickering, complaining, and belittling, will be secure in the love of their Lord.

When I think back to what I heard while growing up in a pastor's home, two voices ring loud and clear in my mind: the strong voice of my dad interceding for his family; and the soft voice of my mother lifting each of us to the throne of grace. Nothing brings a child more security than knowing his parents love God.

Love the Lord fervently. "Love the Lord your God with *all* your heart and with *all* your soul and with *all* your strength" (Deuteronomy 6:5). A half-hearted devotion to God is worse than no devotion at all, especially when we have children watching us. This is where the vast majority go wrong. The essentials of life often crowd out our time with the Lord, the very priority that would straighten out some of the messes we get ourselves into. Without daily family devotions we lose our focus and begin to major on the minors and minor on the majors.

Loving the Lord fervently will result in faithfulness: reading the Word, praying, attending church, and working daily on an ever-growing, ever-deepening relationship with the One we ought to love the most. As our children see such a lifestyle modeled before them, and are included in the process, it will become natural for them to desire a lifestyle that pleases the Lord. This includes their decisions in the type of clothes they wear and the way they wear their hair and makeup.

As a professional athlete turned minister, I am continually amazed when I see grown men play softball or some other sport with all their hearts—diving, sliding, allowing their minds to write checks their bodies can no longer cash—yet they can be so casual in their church attendance, so nonchalant in their approach to their God-given role as high priest of their home. Kenneth Wuest, in his book, *Treasures from the Greek New Testament,* translates 1 John 3:1 to read: "Behold, what *foreign* kind of love is this that the Father has bestowed on us."[3] It has never been uncommon for someone to sacrifice his life for a person or a cause he loved, but it was a foreign kind of love that would sacrifice all for an enemy. Such love could only come from the heart of God. If Jesus was willing to die for me, His most bitter of enemies, one whose very sin nailed Him to the cross, isn't living the rest of my life in a way that pleases Him the very least I can do? If, as parents, we can model before our children exactly what it means to be involved in a meaningful relationship with Jesus, and if we can "pass the baton" from one generation to the next, as Dr. James Dobson states, we can count ourselves successful. If not, then no matter what we accomplish, how much we accumulate, or how great we become, it won't amount to much.

Girls who begin to develop physically and wear revealing clothing send a message that says, "I'm lacking in the love department." Young men who choose hairstyles that go against the status quo shout, "Won't someone please notice me?" Are our teens sending such nonverbal messages to us? Are they crying out for more of our attention even though that would be the last thing they would ever verbalize? Of all we can give them, what they truly desire is *us*.

Jay Kesler, president of Youth for Christ, has edited a book with Ronald A. Beers entitled *Parents & Teenagers*. They describe a well-known play where two boys are standing on the back porch after their father's funeral. They write, "Their father was a salesman who spent all his time traveling and working, always trying to make the big sale. But as the boys look at the cement step that they and their dad built together one Saturday—he had gotten a wheelbarrow and a pile of sand and a shovel and cement and poured it—they say, 'There's more of Dad on this back step than in all the sales he ever made.' This story . . . sums up our society's value structure that makes it easy for us to miss developing relationships. But our most treasured moments come from human relationships, not from worldly success. A boy raised on beans with his father is better off than a boy raised on steak without."[4]

Deep inside, our kids are searching for ways to win our approval, most of the time subconsciously. As we learn to "love the Lord fervently," we will be more relaxed and secure in His unconditional love. Then we'll be better equipped to share that kind of love with our teens; this is exactly what they want and need.

This may be an appropriate time to put this book down and go tap on your teenager's door. If you have fallen short of modeling a genuine love for the Lord, confess that and ask for forgiveness, then have a time of prayer together, simply sharing from your heart. If you've been successful in this area of parenting, continue to affirm your teenager with a warm hug and a prayer of thanksgiving that God gave you the neatest kid in the world.

Teach the young diligently. Much of who we *really* are will be caught by our children, but this certainly doesn't exclude the conscious, consistent transference of God's truth from one generation to another. Teaching Jesus to our youth is primarily the responsibility of the home, not the church or the Christian school. That's not to suggest we teach classes at home; simply follow the scriptural admonition found in Deuteronomy 6:7,8: ". . . talk about them [God's truths] when you sit at home and when you walk along the road, when you lie down and when you get up. Tie them as symbols on your hands and bind them on your foreheads. Write them on the doorframes of your houses and on your gates."

I had the wonderful privilege last year of traveling to Israel. On the plane I sat close to an orthodox Jewish family moving from New York to Israel. Their twelve-year-old son actually wore a little black box, called a phylactery, around his forehead. (See Matthew 23:5.) I don't believe this is quite what the Lord had in mind. Instead, I believe He wants us to make the teaching of His ways fun and natural. It should be comfortable and enjoyable to learn about Jesus, and to include Him in all our conversations. True-to-life Christianity is designed for Tuesday afternoon as well as Sunday morning. In the same way we discuss the weather and how our day went, we should be able to talk about God's presence in our lives and be available to pray about every situation together. As we discuss what's for dinner and whether or not the Phillies won, we might ask, "What's the neatest thing you learned from your Bible reading today?" This isn't a time to lecture, by the way, but to enjoy the Word of God in a practical, naturally flowing conversation.

If you feel inadequate about leading devotions, share your concerns with your kids and ask them to pray for you.

Surprisingly, they'll not respect you less, but more. I've given my daughters permission to ask me if I've spent enough time in prayer on a daily basis. It's amazing how they can pick out the days I haven't.

One evening shortly after dinner I asked my family to gather in the living room for fifteen or twenty minutes for devotions. My teenage daughter had two friends visiting, but family devotions aren't forgotten simply because we have guests. I wanted to discuss a sermon our pastor had preached on "contemptible familiarity," or how Jesus was just too familiar to the people in Nazareth for them to accept Him. I asked the girls to name some things that have become so familiar we no longer appreciate them. They gave answers on everything from basic necessities such as food, clothing, and shelter to praying over food at mealtimes. Then we began to realize how easy it is to take the Lord's presence in our lives for granted. This led, oddly enough, to a discussion about love, sex, and dating. What began as a simple discussion ended up in an hour of practical instruction. We concluded our time together by praying that all of us would learn to practice and enjoy the Lord's presence continually, and not take it for granted. My wife Pam even included prayer for all the girl's future husbands. It was fun; it was natural; it was powerful.

Fear the Lord greatly. What we've discussed so far in this chapter can be summarized in three simple words: fear the Lord. One precept builds upon another. If we truly learn to fear the Lord, to reverence His holy name, we will always prefer His will above our own.

Somehow we must grow to enjoy the built-in consciousness that reassures us His eyes are ever upon us. He's watching us. He sees. He knows. He understands. He's not waiting to pounce on us every time we make a mistake, but

He's a kind and loving Shepherd who cares for His sheep. Once we fully understand this, we will *hear,* we will *love,* we will *teach.* And, if our kids learn to respect and revere their heavenly Father, then clothes, hair, and makeup styles won't become an issue.

The ancient Hebrew scribes would not spell the entire name of Yahweh. They would pen only the consonants YHWH, and only after they washed their entire body. Can you imagine taking a bath or shower before mentioning God's name? That seems impractical, but wouldn't our children benefit if we had that kind of attitude toward our Lord?

During my first year with the Phillies, I had the privilege of playing on the same team with Ryne Sandberg and Jorge Bell. Both were fresh out of high school, and Jorge had recently come to the States from his home in the Dominican Republic. He knew very little English at the time. In fact, the only English words he knew were not worth repeating. He already knew how to take God's name in vain, though I don't believe he knew what he was saying. Since I speak *muy piquito Espanol,* I taught Jorge some decent English words. The next time he felt like cursing he blurted out, "Praise the Lord and God bless you!" Our teammates were stunned, to say the least. Wouldn't it be wonderful if we could influence those around us, including kids, who take God's name in vain to turn their words into praises?

One thing I agonize over is the notion that our youth are losing the fear of the Lord, just like the stiff-necked Israelites to whom these four keys were originally given. It's not difficult to imagine what lies ahead for us if we don't learn, corporately and individually, to once again fear the Lord. The place to begin is in our homes.

We need to ask ourselves, "What is being *heard* in our homes? Are we sincerely *loving* the Lord with all our hearts? What are we *teaching* our family? Do we *fear* the Lord?" If we diligently seek to implement God's commands, the end result will be a family that knows how to make the right decision. And making right decisions is critical when dealing with issues like clothes, hair, and makeup.

WHO'S AT THE WHEEL?

Now we're ready to talk french fries! The desire of every godly parent should be that our children grow up learning to make righteous decisions on their own. God knows we can't be there to make every decision for them; only He can. So the sooner a desire is created within them to discover the way they should go, through the natural kind of training we've been talking about (see Proverbs 22:6), the better.

The rubber really meets the road during the adolescent years when they start making choices for themselves. "Because I'm the mommy" works great for a two-year-old, but our teens need a more complete explanation. The proverbial generation gap is really a gap in communication. "Because I said so" needs to be more clearly defined. When your fifteen-year-old comes out of her room dressed in a skirt that's too short, she needs to know that she looks wonderful, and that boys are certainly going to notice her . . . but for the wrong reason.

Remember, a heavy fog rolls over our kids during the junior high years (ages twelve to fourteen), so don't expect them to understand what you're talking about. Continue, gently but firmly, to guide them along, much like the fog horn that helps the ship steer clear of unseen obstacles. Getting angry and making an issue of these situations isn't the most effective way to teach our children. As maturity sets in, they'll begin to understand and be thankful that we cared enough to be there through the painful, confusing transition from childhood to adulthood.

Parents who establish boundaries, then relax them as time goes by, will enjoy the respect and friendship of their adult children. However, parents who enforce rigid boundaries or no boundaries at all will find their adult children have very little respect for them.

As a youth pastor, I once had a parent march her teenage son into my office and say, "Pastor Randy, Johnny wants to go to the school dance. I told him we would do whatever you told him."

I asked, "Johnny, do you really want to go to that dance?"

"Oh, yeah, Pastor Randy. All my friends are going to be there," he said.

"Okay, go ahead," I replied, "but first, let's ask the Holy Spirit, who lives inside you, whether or not He'll be pleased if you go. The day after the dance, call me and we'll talk about the experience."

We prayed and I dismissed Johnny . . . so I could calm down his mother. She couldn't believe I had given permission for him to go, and she was upset. I assured her he'd have found a creative way to be there; this way we could find out whether or not the years of Christian training had paid off.

The most common mistake I've seen Christian parents make is their inability to let go. Smothered teens generally participate in some pretty wild stuff once they are out on their own because they don't know how to handle freedom. The healthiest teens I work with are those whose parents let go little by little and increasingly trust their teens with responsibility rewarded by privilege. My oldest brother once let his seventeen-year-old daughter travel with her girlfriend to Europe. I was astonished and asked how he could possibly allow her such freedom. He said, "The same love that causes you to want to hold on tightly is that which also releases you to let go."

Our teenagers need to have the freedom to make some choices we may not approve of, especially when it deals with an area on which the Bible is silent. One of the most valuable lessons our children can learn is how to discern, and then obey, the still, small voice that speaks to us from deep within. When that happens, we can say the baton has safely been passed. And we'll be able to say, along with the apostle John, "I have no greater joy than to hear that my children are walking in the truth" (3 John 4).

THE WEAPON OF PRAYER

Again, some type of extreme in our outward appearance is more than likely a signal of inner conflict. The apostle Peter's admonition still rings true today: "Your beauty should not come from outward adornment, such as braided hair and the wearing of gold jewelry and fine clothes. Instead, it should be that of your inner self, the unfading beauty of a gentle and quiet spirit, which is of great worth in God's sight" (1 Peter 3:3,4).

The women of that day often wore elaborate, time-consuming hairstyles, and Peter warned them against extremes to keep their external and internal beauty in balance. In no way was he saying to neglect the outward appearance. As Chuck Swindoll writes in *Strike the Original Match,* "If the house needs painting, paint it."[5]

How should parents handle a teenager who displays extreme signs in their choice of clothing, hair, and makeup? Carefully and *prayerfully.* Talk to your heavenly Father about the concerns you have for your son or daughter. And ask for wisdom on how to approach the matter. Then carefully communicate with them, politely asking questions that will help you understand what is at the root of the problem.

There's no way to over-emphasize the importance of intercessory prayer for our children. Remember, "We wrestle not against flesh and blood, but against principalities, against powers, against the rulers of the darkness of this world, against spiritual wickedness in high places" (Ephesians 6:12, KJV). There's a battle raging for the souls of our kids, and Satan is a formidable foe. But take courage in knowing that "greater is He who is in you than he who is in the world" (1 John 4:4, NASB), or as one great preacher said, "Greater is He that is in you than he that is chasing you!" He has given us "authority . . . to overcome all the power of the enemy" (Luke 10:19). Cling to His promise that "the God of peace shall bruise Satan under your feet shortly" (Romans 16:20, KJV).

Dave Erickson, a young man who grew up in my youth group, went through a rebellious time trying to find himself as a sixteen-year-old. I took him to lunch one day and said, "Dave, you can run as far away from God as you like, but you'll never get away from Him . . . because you have a praying mother." Not only is Dave serving the Lord today, but he and his wife are in full-time ministry and sense the call of God on their lives to serve as foreign missionaries.

No matter what signals you may be receiving through your teen's clothes, hair, or makeup, don't give up. Right now your kids may be struttin' and strollin', rockin' and rollin', or stylin' and profilin'. Declare by faith, as Joshua did, "As for me and my house, we will serve the Lord" (Joshua 24:15, KJV) by *hearing* the truth continually, *loving* the Lord fervently, *teaching* the young diligently, and *fearing* the Lord greatly.

The Reverend Randy Greer is currently serving as senior associate at Trinity Life Center in Las Vegas, Nevada. After graduating from Southern California College in 1978, Pastor Greer was drafted by the Philadelphia Phillies and played in their organization for three years. He then spent ten years of ministry at Full Gospel Assembly of God in Bell Gardens, California before moving to Las Vegas.

He and his wife Pamela have three daughters: Brandie, Ashley, and Lindsey.

15

Movies, Music, and More

LYNN WHEELER

As an evangelist, I have spoken to thousands of young people at camps, retreats, and conventions. Time and again, one question arises from pastors, youth pastors, and parents: "Why do our youth get fired up for God at camps and conventions, then within a few weeks after coming back home, the enthusiasm fades?" Youth leaders have tried everything to make the camp-convention experience continue at home. And, in fact, in some places revival fires continue year around.

Why does this camp-convention-home phenomena occur? Perhaps our young people pursue God more in these settings because, for a week, they are separated from radio and television. Usually, camp rules forbid listening to the radio and watching television, for it is believed that listening to the wrong kinds of music and watching ungodly movies take away from their time and quest for God. I believe there's a lesson to be learned here.

Today's youth face many obstacles in their attempt to serve the Lord. We live in an age when we must continue to preach the Word of God to our young people, and, at the same time, remove as many obstacles as possible. Movies and music are obstacles we cannot ignore. Is there anything of value young people are learning from the music they listen to and the movies they see? It's naive to suggest they aren't learning something.

Our youth are greatly affected by what they watch. Violent and sexually explicit scenes *do* have an impact and often produce negative behavior. Likewise, music that promotes rebellion and ungodliness is assimilated and acted out by many teens and young adults.

Over lunch one day, a church leader shared a personal incident that reveals the power and influence of television. He said he was watching a television drama in which a man chased another man with a knife. When the pursuer caught his prey, he stabbed his victim repeatedly. During the scene, my friend's four-year-old daughter was playing quietly in the same room. During a commercial, the little girl walked into the kitchen, took a knife out of the drawer, walked back into the room, and tried to stab her dad. Tragedy was avoided only because she stabbed with the wrong end of the knife.

After retrieving the knife, he scolded his daughter and tried to collect his thoughts, but this real life drama left him shaken. At the time, this was not a Christian home, but this father recognized the potential danger of Hollywood's invasion. Thereafter, he enforced a rigid set of guidelines for television viewing in his household.

Do parents have a right to monitor what their child is watching? Absolutely! In one of the messages in a tape series I produced on the family, I list "monitoring the media" as a key responsibility of parents.

The youth of this generation are saturated with things that are detrimental to their spiritual life. Satan is subtle, often appearing as an "angel of light" (2 Corinthians 11:14). He goes about "like a roaring lion, seeking whom he may devour" (1 Peter 5:8, NKJV). Through music, movies, and ungodly magazines, the enemy, subtly or otherwise, attempts to gain a stronghold on our young people. We won't give him a stronghold, but sometimes we give him a foothold by allowing our youth to indulge in unhealthy entertainment. And if we give the devil a foothold, you can be sure he'll take a stronghold. It's up to us, as parents and Christian leaders, to pull our youth from the jaws of the enemy.

Take a moment to do an inventory. Consider how movies, music, and other attractions influence your household. Remember, our youth follow what their parents *do* more than what they *say*. If parents and church leaders want their youth to live in victory in these areas, they must be taught by example.

In the Old Testament we read about the importance of passing values down from generation to generation, the greatest being the desire to do what is right in the sight of God. The areas discussed below are greatly influencing our youth today. It is time for us to take a long, hard look at the movies, music, and pornography that are drawing them away from God.

AT THE MOVIES

I was raised in church during a time when *everything* was considered a sin. All we heard was what *not* to do and where *not* to go. One of the leading "thou shalt nots" when I was a teenager ended with "go to the movies." Selective viewing wasn't an option. We simply didn't go. Today, that teaching isn't as prevalent, but there's still cause for concern. With the advent of the VCR, movie viewing has become a convenient, inexpensive form of recreation. Unfortunately, movies we wouldn't allow our children to go to a theater to see or go to ourselves are easily rented and viewed without enforced discretion. But it's important to consider that God is concerned about what we watch. The psalmist provides guidelines for our viewing habits: "Turn my eyes away from worthless things . . ."(Psalm 119:37) and "I will set before my eyes no vile thing" (Psalm 101:3). Webster defines *vile* as "morally base or evil; wicked and sinful; offensive to the senses," and *worthless* as "having no value, dignity, virtue, etc." That reminds us of Philippians 4:8: "Finally, brethren, whatsoever things are true, whatsoever things are honest, whatsoever things are just, whatsoever things are pure, whatsoever things are lovely, whatsoever things are of good report; if there be any virtue, and if there be any praise, think on these things" (KJV).

Most of us are guilty of spending an extended amount of time watching worthless programming. Then when it's over, we wonder why we wasted our time. But a worse tragedy is that we have chosen to set before our eyes wicked things, programs that promote sinful activities and attitudes. Whether we watch them in the movie theater or in the privacy of our own home, the fact cannot be ignored: these shows are negatively impacting our society, especially our youth. Christians, young or old, should not only be uncomfortable with Hollywood's use of profanity, sex, and violence, but they should be convicted if they partake.

Michael Medved, co-host of The Public Broadcasting System's "Sneak Previews," was interviewed by Michael G. Maudlin for an article in *Christianity Today*. The subject of the interview was Medved's book, *Hollywood vs. America*. As a result of his book, he has been called a "secret Christian," and has received anonymous, threatening phone calls for saying, "Movies today are bad, immoral, perhaps dangerous, and certainly not friendly to religion or traditional values."[1]

One of the themes of *Hollywood vs. America* is that the film industry is out of touch with the rest of the country. The Associated Press poll found that eighty percent of Americans think there is too much profanity in films, eighty-two percent think there is too much violence, and seventy-two percent feel there is too much sex.[2] I applaud America. It's time we stand up for what we believe. We must do all we can to take back the minds of our youth. They're receiving a perverted message from Hollywood. We must launch a counter-assault if we're to win the war being waged against godly values.

TOO MUCH SEX

In an interview with *Christianity Today*, Medved made a valid observation: "... the only kind of sex that is forbidden on TV and in the movies is sex between husband and wife. On screen, sex occurs mostly among single people, usually teenagers."[3] In addition, he writes in his book, "On TV, references to sex outside marriage are fourteen times more common than sex inside marriage."[4]

Statistics continue to suggest a rise in the number of teenagers experimenting with sex before marriage. If that is true, then America's moral decline is escalating. Not even the AIDS epidemic appears to be slowing it down. Today's generation of young people, like others before it, has been entangled in the "if it feels good, do it" philosophy. As reported by the Center for Population Options, "... by age twenty, seventy-five percent of females and eighty-six percent of males are sexually active. The percentage of never-married fifteen to nineteen-year-old females reporting sexual activity rose from forty-two percent in 1982 to 49.5 percent in 1988, the most recent year for which data is available. In 1988, sixty percent of fifteen- to nineteen-year-old males reported sexual activity. Twenty-six percent of females report having had sexual intercourse by age fifteen. Twenty-six percent of white males, thirty-three percent of Hispanic males, and sixty-nine percent of black males report having had sex by age fifteen. The center also reported that two and one half million adolescents are infected with sexually transmitted diseases annually. From 1960 to 1988 the prevalence of gonorrhea among fifteen to nineteen-year-olds increased by 170 percent, more than quadruple the rate of increase among twenty to twenty-four-year-olds. The study also revealed that more than one-fifth of the people with AIDS are in their twenties. Because the latency period between HIV infection and onset of symptoms is about ten years, most were infected as adolescents. Also, the reported cases of AIDS among adolescents increased twenty-nine percent between July 1990 and July 1991. In 1986 AIDS was the seventh leading cause of death among fifteen- to twenty-four-year-olds; in 1987, it climbed to the sixth leading cause."[5]

Lust is one of Satan's most powerful weapons. Our kids do not need Hollywood's help. There is hardly a movie released without a steamy sex scene, mostly between two people not married to each other. Once we were spared all this by watching the major networks. Now that too has changed.

The Word of God still lists sexual immorality as an act of the sinful nature. (See Galatians 5:19.) If young people watch shows with nudity and sex scenes, lust is inevitable. When lust dominates, people act without thinking.

Don't give in to the temptation to watch sexual acts on the movie screen. We and our children must stand on the Word of God. "It is God's will that you should be holy; that you should avoid sexual immorality; that each of you should learn to control his own body in a way that is holy and honorable, not in passionate lust like the heathen, who do not know God . . ." (1 Thessalonians 4:3-5).

THE "ART" OF VIOLENCE

Hollywood not only bombards its viewers with sexually explicit content, but violence within the media of film has increased dramatically in recent years. Michael Medved states: "In movies and on TV, violence is used to solve every problem; it is also presented as the essence of sexual attractiveness for a male."[6] That's no surprise to anyone who views contemporary movies. Hollywood promotes the tough guy. The message is: if you don't like someone, fight or, better yet, kill. Hollywood's solution to every problem is violence. Even women and children are sometimes portrayed as cold-blooded killers.

It's no wonder our youth have trouble handling their problems. Scriptwriters fail to teach young people how to cope with crises in a peaceful way. Why? Because Hollywood doesn't believe a movie will make money without violence. Medved writes: "If you look at all the movies released since 1983, PG-rated movies did almost twice as well as R-rated movies; in 1991, they did three times as well."[7] Yet, Hollywood continues to produce R-rated movies with excessive violence. Inordinate violence turns young men into fighters who believe physical confrontation is the only way to solve a problem. We need to turn off the violence that has invaded our homes by way of television.

We can no longer pretend it's not harming us or our children.

An article by James Dobson, president of Focus on the Family, warned of the new programs approved for air time. Dr. Dobson shared about such violence as a cop being kicked, stabbed, and shot to death. Another show depicted a Texas police officer killing a suspected drug dealer. Television constantly portrays racial hatred and gut-wrenching violence. Blood baths and shooting sprees have become so common we are almost numb to them.[8]

A twenty-two-year investigation was conducted at the University of Illinois, Chicago. According to psychologist Leonard Eron, 875 subjects from a semi-rural New York county were accepted for study when they were eight years old. By the time they were thirty years old, those who had watched the most television violence had been convicted of a significantly larger number of serious crimes. They had learned not to feel compassion for the suffering of others. The examiners concluded the human mind is capable of such adaptation when exposed habitually to violent acts. Eron, who headed the American Psychological Association's Commission on Violence and Youth, concluded, "Television violence affects youngsters of all ages, of both genders, at all socioeconomic levels, and all levels of intelligence, and the effect is not limited to children who are already disposed to being aggressive and is not restricted to this country."[9]

PROFANITY

Children learn to speak by repeating what they hear. The learning process is not limited to parental input, and continues into the teenage years. Unfortunately, much of what is heard doesn't reflect the values parents try to impart. Time and again, I have been around parents when their child says something unacceptable. The question is always asked: "Where did you hear that?" Two different answers seem to be common. Either they heard it from a friend, or they heard it on television. The film industry has provided our youth with many heroes, making idols out of fictitious characters. Our young people begin to emulate them, which includes talking like them. It is estimated that seventy-two percent of teens mimic what they see. Perhaps as many mimic what they hear.

We can go hardly anywhere without hearing profanity and people taking God's name in vain. We don't have control over what others say, but we do have control over what we choose to watch. The onslaught of profanity should make every Christian cringe, and God forbid that we should ever become used to it.

It is estimated that eighty-nine percent of teenagers list their favorite activity as movie-going or video-watching. Ted Baehr of Christian Film and Television says, "The average teen in the USA watches fifty R-rated videos, plus fifty R-rated feature films per year."[10] And note, that does not include morally unacceptable television shows.

Medved, in an article written for *Focus on the Family*, said, "We must hope and work for an attitude adjustment that goes beyond a temporary shift in marketplace strategies. In the same way that we ask major corporations to take greater responsibility for polluting our air and water, it is entirely appropriate that concerned Americans take up a long-term effort to demand that our huge entertainment conglomerates demonstrate a new accountability for their pollution of the cultural atmosphere that we all breathe."[11]

In *Christianity Today,* Medved concluded, "I don't think I can review movies much longer. It is an assault on the senses, and an assault on the spirit."[12]

MTV AND MUSIC

Another attack against our youth is being waged by the music industry. The word *influence* is defined as "an act bringing about a result without the use of force or authority." Nothing describes music and its demi-gods more accurately. Music plays a major part in our lives. It moves our emotions and stirs our spirits. Contemporary worship music fills our sanctuaries and puts us in a spirit of worship; I wouldn't want to have church without it. But music designed to send negative messages, even anti-social messages, is mass produced by the music industry.

In her book, *Raising PG Kids in an X-Rated Society,* Tipper Gore shares a letter that she and sixteen wives of U. S. representatives and senators wrote on May 31, 1985: "It is our concern that some of the music which the recording industry sells today increasingly portrays explicit sex and violence, and glorifies the use of drugs and alcohol. It is indiscriminately available to persons of any age through record stores and the media."[13]

A good amount of secular music in America propagates the same message as movies. The power of the video age has put music and visualization together. "MTV, the cable music television network, heightened adult concern over the content of songs and videos broadcast on radio and TV," states Larry E. Greeson, Department of Educational Psychology, Miami University.[14] Robert Pittman, vice president of programming for MTV, said, "At MTV we don't shoot for the fourteen year olds. We own them."[15]

A book entitled *Social Learning Theory* claims, "Electronic media, TV in particular, have been cited as social learning factors influencing the attitudes, values, and behavior patterns of young people."[16] That frightens me when I hear the secular music being sung by the teens I've ridden with to camps and retreats. Churched teens are as familiar with secular music as their unchurched peers. I'm equally disturbed to know that many of them watch MTV regularly. "Content analyses have indicated that adolescent behaviors such as sex-role stereotyping, aggression, drug use, and sexual activities appear as frequent themes on both network television and MTV."[17]

Time magazine reported how cult leader David Koresh inserted MTV into his daily schedule. Once in the cult, Davidians surrendered their rights to watch television, while their leader watched it frequently. This is indicative of the connection between physical aggression, sexual aggression, and rock music. *Time* reported that growing up, ". . . Koresh was . . . an indifferent student (rebellious inclination), but an avid reader of the Bible who prayed for hours and memorized long passages of Scripture." He was also an accomplished rock guitarist. He played guitar ". . . using rock music . . . to recruit followers."[18] While MTV cannot be blamed for the tragic episode in Waco, Texas that shocked our nation, it may have influenced the mind of the primary player.

MTV *can* be credited as a major contributor to the success of many heavy metal groups. In 1989, the group Guns-N-Roses reported a two-year income of more than $20 million. Jeffrey Arnett, Ph.D., University of Chicago stated, "The concerts are expensive (typically about $20), and many subjects reported spending money on expensive t-shirts (also about $20) and programs ($10-$15) at the concerts, in addition to their regular expenditures on recordings. On average, they reported spending $38.70 a month on music-related purchases."[19] Perhaps even more alarming, according to Arnett, was ". . . their identification with the music and the performers as remarkably strong; when attending concerts, many of them envisioned themselves on the stage, as a romantic dream or a fervent ambition."[20] If the same dollars were spent on Christian music and t-shirts, a positive message would reach many kids.

Not all secular music is "bad" music, and not all music labeled "gospel" is good music. However, if we dig through the garbage can to find food, we'll experience a lot of bad before we get to the good. If there is a problem in your home with rebellion or over-aggressiveness, find out what your teenager is listening to. Replace unholy music with godly music. Be assured it will create a better atmosphere in your home.

There is a program called "Back in Control" (BIC) that provides workshops for families that focus on teaching parenting skills. "In order to regain control, BIC advocates that parents set very clear and specific rules for their children and consistently follow through in enforcement of them."[21] Tipper Gore stated, ". . . the teen years are turning points in young lives. Teenagers are endowed with the emotions, passions, and physical capabilities of adults, without the adult judgment to harness them. Because of the pressures they face, they may need even more quality time from parents. Teens look to their parents for a moral compass, values, and ethical advice they can apply to romances and friendships."[22]

Our kids desperately need adult attention. They want us to know and love them for who they are. Though it's a well-used cliche, ask yourself: "Have I hugged my child today?"

PORNOGRAPHIC POISON

In his article, "Pornography and Sexual Violence: Booming Business Victimizing Children, Women and Men," Nelson Price states: "Pornography has found or created a tremendous audience in this country, and has mushroomed into an estimated $8 billion per year business."[23] Unfortunately, that audience consists of teens as well as adults, but pornographers are unconcerned with those their product reaches or the detrimental effect it has on our society.

Most young boys become inquisitive about sex during early adolescence. Sometimes out of fear or embarrassment they're reluctant to ask questions and choose to explore for themselves. Dr. Dobson states ". . . few people realize how incredibly addictive pornography is to most boys during early adolescence. One exposure at just the right time can capture a susceptible young man on the verge of manhood. He then begins a masturbatory habit that feeds on ever more explicit and violent material."[24]

Pornography is progressive in nature. Photographs and erotic literature suffice for a while, but they soon lose their power. Then they must become more erotic to produce the same excitement. The addiction can, and often does, escalate into rape and other violent crimes. The destructive power of pornography received national attention when convicted killer Ted Bundy granted Dr. Dobson an exclusive interview. Bundy told how pornography had gripped him as a young boy and fueled his fantasies to brutalize women. By the time Bundy was executed in Florida State Prison, he had raped and killed at least twenty-eight women and girls.

If you find pornography in your child's possession, don't panic. Confront them and communicate honestly and lovingly. Let them know the potential dangers. Then pray with them that God would help them lose their attraction for it before it becomes an addiction.

LIVE BY THE SPIRIT

The issues discussed in this chapter are problems our youth have to deal with daily. They're faced with decisions about what movies to watch, what music to listen to, and whether or not to be sexually active all in the light of what their peers are doing. These ongoing obstacles become ongoing challenges for parents and those in youth leadership. The best way I know to fight the battle is with the Word of God. Scripture admonishes: "Live by the Spirit, and you will not gratify the desires of the sinful nature. For the sinful nature desires what is contrary to the Spirit . . ." (Galatians 5:16,17).

As parents, we have a biblical mandate to obtain and maintain a wholesome atmosphere in our homes. We must control the television set, play godly music, and challenge our kids with Christian reading. Parenting has never been more difficult. If we'll turn our home and our children over to God and allow Him to reside there we'll have hope . . . and answers.

The Reverend Lynn Wheeler graduated from Central Bible College in 1982 with a B. A. in Biblical Studies. For two years he traveled as an evangelist, then served as a youth pastor until 1989, first at Park Crest Assembly of God in Springfield, Missouri, then at Crossroads Cathedral in Oklahoma City. Lynn returned to evangelism and speaks at youth camps and conventions, singles conferences, retreats, and crusades.

SPIRITUAL LIFE

A man's Sunday self and his weekly self are like two halves of a round trip ticket—not good if detached.

Anonymous

16

God, Kids, and Youth Ministry

MICHAEL DE VITO

"No way! I'm never going back! It's boring and everyone's stuck up!" Perhaps your teenager has made such comments about his or her youth group at church. Students' complaints range from feeling as if they have no friends at church, to "church is no fun," to "all they do is play games." Inevitably, the phone rings and Mrs. Smith says, "Pastor Mike, Frank doesn't like coming to youth group anymore. Can you help me?"

If you've experienced this scenario, you're not alone. We can't ignore the problem. So how do we instill a love for church in our kids? Both parents and the church must take responsibility for finding the answer.

A CONCEPT OF GOD

A church youth ministry exists to help students understand who God is. Our job is to help them realize they can have a personal relationship with an awesome God. Unfortunately, many teenagers believe God is either a "cosmic kill-joy" or a type of Santa Claus. Scripture teaches that nothing could be further from the truth. Instead, God is the life-giver. Without Him we could do nothing.

Teens need to understand their desperate need for a personal relationship with Jesus Christ. The average teenager feels invincible and believes he has no need for God. Maybe later, but not now. A series of tragedies brought the kids in our church face to face with reality. After losing four students in two years—one to a brain tumor, two in an automobile accident, and one who was brutally murdered—our youth have learned that life and friendships are to be valued. When life's storms turned their world upside down, they were eager to discuss their need for God and each other.

Whatever crises they face, our kids need to know the body of Christ is a place where they can find safety, refuge, and answers to life's most pressing questions. The church should provide an atmosphere in which students are challenged to know what they believe and why they believe it; challenged to put their faith in action through service and missions projects; challenged to know Christ and make Christ known. The church is where the body of Christ comes together to celebrate and be equipped and trained for service.

HOME AND CHURCH

Parents set the tone for the type of church experience their children have today. In raising my two children, I've wanted them to view the church as an exciting and fun place. They've been told they will only get out of it what they put into it. But that starts with my attitude as a parent.

What do I model for them? Do I love going to church? Do I practice what I preach? Am I consistent in my Christian walk?

Many young people have been turned off to church because of their parents' negative attitudes. Sunday afternoon was the time to pick apart the sermon and criticize what they didn't like. Negative attitudes breed negative attitudes. Parents who complain about the church need not wonder why their kids turn their backs on God, while those who find an area of service and worship God with a positive attitude will be far more successful in keeping their kids turned on to God.

YOUTH MINISTRY

What can youth workers do to build a positive concept of God in kids and support the efforts of parents? The life of the typical teenager can be described in one word: "busy." Their distractions can be negative or positive, but they're distractions just the same. The church youth group is just one more activity vying for their attention, but it must be perceived by them as one of the most important appointments of their weekly schedule if they're to stay plugged in. The church youth ministry must assist in laying the right kind of foundation for a teen to build his or her life upon, creating the right atmosphere for emotional and spiritual growth.

What do teens see, hear, and feel when they walk into their church or youth service? Does the atmosphere communicate their importance? Are they accepted? Loved? Welcome? One of the greatest needs of youth is to have a place where they feel a part of something they can give their life to and feel a sense of belonging. If a youth ministry is providing this sense of purpose, it's providing a great service.

The youth ministry of a local church can be one of the most influential aspects of our children's spiritual life. Here are some characteristics of an effective youth ministry:

Creating the atmosphere. Growing up in the home of a public school teacher, I spent many hours working in my dad's classroom to help him create the right atmosphere for motivating his students. We created a bulletin board that taught various concepts and informed the students of monthly events. Those experiences have affected what I've tried to create for my youth ministry. We recently completed a new youth center that broadcasts: "This is a place for teens!" When students walk in they are overwhelmed with four twenty-six-inch television monitors and a large screen that display music, sports, cartoon, and worship videos. As they watch the videos, they can enjoy food from a snack bar that offers everything from donuts to bagel-dogs. From the meeting room to the sports page on specially designed bulletin boards in the guys' restroom, the facility says, "This is where it's happening, come be a part!" In addition, as teens look around the room they are challenged with various service opportunities, such as feeding the homeless, working at the children's hospital, praying, and working on a nationwide youth crisis telephone hotline.

Although the building is a great resource tool, it must be more than videos, music, snack bars, and posters promoting the next big event. God's presence, passion, and power must be felt and experienced, or all is in vain. We want teens to be less impressed with our facility and more impressed by God and His desire to be their personal friend. The atmosphere that's been created merely points them to an awareness of God. The Bible says if God is lifted up He will draw all men to Himself. (See John 12:32.) As God is lifted up, keeping kids in church will not be a problem. In fact, they will want to arrive early and stay late.

Student ownership. "Give it away" should be the theme of every youth ministry. It's time for youth ministry to be placed within the hands of some of the most talented, gifted, and creative people around: junior and senior high school students. Teens will be a part of what they own. They'll be more excited about what they have created. Their potential will be tapped only when we put cameras, paint brushes, scripts, instruments, and Bibles in their hands.

Five years ago I was without a worship team. I pulled out my wife's old guitar, blew off the dust, and began to play my three favorite chords: D, G, and A, adding an occasional Em and C. Somehow through my feeble attempt to lead worship, I inspired students to try themselves. They responded by saying, "Hey, if Mike can do it, we can." They now have taken ownership of the worship band. Keeping these kids in church hasn't been a problem. They're thrilled at the opportunity to lead worship, whether it's before a handful or thousands.

Allow teens to make mistakes as they learn to put their faith into action. After all, if there's any place they should feel free to fail, it's in the church. Our future leaders may stumble and fall along the way, but before long we'll find them serving on the mission field, pastoring their own churches, administering large events, producing and directing videos, and serving as youth ministers. A teen who feels free to make mistakes will be more attracted to service. Parents, it's time to call your kids from the sidelines and encourage them to get in the game. There's no doubt they can do it.

SERVICE AND MISSIONS

The church has often neglected to call teens to service. Athletic coaches and band teachers can ask them to go the second mile; why not the church? We are now seeing youth ministries move from being a glorified YMCA to strategic equipping centers where teens are putting their faith into action. A youth ministry with a heart for service projects and missions trips will be a growing, healthy youth ministry. It will change lives and make an impact around the world. Our kids want to serve; we need to provide them with meaningful opportunities.

In our church, November is devoted to encouraging teens to understand the heartbeat of God through service and missions projects. We've found ourselves downtown feeding the homeless and walking the halls of a local children's hospital, ministering to terminally ill kids. Our teens have also had an opportunity to answer crisis hotline phone calls and lead individuals into a relationship with Jesus Christ. We've found ourselves ministering in the inner city of Los Angeles, visiting a small village in Tijuana, and leading an evangelistic crusade in Guatemala. God has used these activities to shape the hearts of our teens.

A few years ago I put a thirteen-year-old on an airplane for her first missions trip. She took up the challenge we had presented. She was on her way to another part of the world to be used by God to change lives. She returned to find her own life had been changed.

REAL ISSUES

Keeping teens in church is a weekly challenge. Youth ministry must be more than fun and games. Real issues must be addressed. Teens are longing for honest answers to life's difficult questions. As parents and youth workers, we must face the issues head on. We cannot hide our heads and pretend, for example, that AIDS will just go away. Relationships, fears and joys, the future, and life's fatal flaws must be addressed from a spiritual, rather than a secular, perspective. God's Word is relevant for every issue our teens face. We need to help them realize it. As we interact in their lives, we must not lose sight of our primary mission: to lead them to a personal relationship with Jesus Christ—not because *we* believe, but because they do.

MAKING MEMORIES

Youth ministry is about creating memories. Relational memories are the most important: between teens; between parents and teens; between the church and teens; and most importantly, between God and teens. Most of us can remember those who had a profound effect on our lives. We'll never be the same because they were there: when major decisions needed to be made, when we faced a difficulty, when we just needed a friend. They helped us make right choices and picked us up when we made wrong ones. Now it's our turn to do the same for a new generation. We can be a part of creating memories that will keep them excited about their involvement in church.

Youth retreats can provide a great atmosphere for making memories. Teens arrive on Monday with physical and emotional baggage, and by Friday they leave a little lighter because God has done a work in their lives. They'll never be the same.

Deuteronomy 4:9 advises, "Be careful, and watch yourselves closely so that you do not forget the things your eyes have seen or let them slip from your heart as long as you live. Teach them to your children and to their children after them."

It's time to create memories for a new generation.

Keeping teens in church and in communion with God is first the responsibility of parents. Then the church comes alongside with youth workers, atmosphere, and programs to do its part. But, ultimately, God is the one who draws us all. As we are reminded in Zechariah 4:6, it's not by our might or by our power, but by His Spirit that ministry is accomplished. We are merely instruments.

The Reverend Michael De Vito has been involved in youth ministry for more than fifteen years. He was youth pastor at The People's Church in Salem, Oregon for seven years before moving to San Diego First Assembly where he ministered for seven years. He is currently Southern California Coordinator for the National Network of Youth Ministries.

He and his wife Kristi have been married for seventeen years. They have two daughters: Candice, age thirteen, and Kimberly, age ten.

17
Keeping Kids in Church
GLENN R. EMBREE

I met a family in the foyer of our church one morning after worship service. They had just moved to our city and had expressed interest in attending our church regularly. The parents were pleasant and eager to introduce me to their son Danny who was about to enter junior high school. Over the next couple of months Danny participated in every youth event that we had to offer: summer camp, fall youth retreat, Friday youth nights, and even our home Bible studies. He seemed to enjoy the youth group and fit in well with his peers. A few months later, I received a phone call from his mother. Danny's interest in church activities had declined dramatically, and every Sunday brought a major confrontation over his church attendance.

I recall another incident where a young girl was brought into my office by her parents. It was one of the most difficult counseling sessions I can remember. Her interest in church had hit an all-time low, so our conversation was awkward and strained.

Through the years I've received phone calls from parents who did not attend our church or, for that matter, any church. They call out of concern for a teenage son or daughter who is running with the wrong crowd, missing curfew, failing at school. A few years ago, a mother called and told me about the difficulty she was having controlling her son. Then she put him on the phone to "talk with the priest." Needless to say, it was a one-sided conversation.

Situations like these are sadly common among parents of teenagers who are no longer interested in church. Some of the stories are tragic. Others may be less serious, but they still upset the family equilibrium. Although their stories and circumstances may vary, the question they pose is always the same: "How do I keep my kids in church?"

IT'S JUST A STAGE

When discussing kids and church, some parents quote Proverbs 22:6: "Train a child in the way he should go, and when he is old he will not turn from it," and take a hands-off approach. Others believe when children challenge their family's Christian standards and various aspects of church life, "it's just a stage that all kids go through," and suggest parents allow it to run its course. Patience and time may be the answer in some cases, but I've seen the "stage" extend beyond high school years into adulthood, and many end up raising their own children outside of church.

The Bible talks about the training of children in relation to their spiritual development. In Hebrew society childhood lasted until adulthood. In contemporary Western culture, we've modified the transition from childhood to adulthood by inserting an indeterminate period of time called *adolescence*. So when can we consider the spiritual training of our children complete?

The training of a child is generally understood to continue until the individual is ready to take on the responsibilities of adult life. During the adolescent or teenage period, parents should not take a hands-off approach to spiritual matters. Nowhere in Scripture are parents encouraged to stand back and observe from a distance. That would only produce disastrous, long-term results. Imagine raising your family on a twenty-six-foot boat. Undoubtedly, you would keep your children right beside you on deck. But, as your children reached their teen years and started pressing for "their own space," you would probably let them sit in a small dinghy securely attached to the back of the boat. What would you do, however, if, half way across the Pacific, they started nagging you for more freedom? Would you cut them adrift, saying, "It's okay. They're heading in the right direction"? Of course not. In the same way, the spiritual line needs to remain attached.

PARENTAL RESPONSIBILITY

Many churches today have youth groups with youth pastors, junior high pastors, and even a youth bus or two. They provide activities and outings for every age group, so how could a child lose interest in church? It's hard to understand, but it happens regularly in every denomination and in every size church. So who is responsible for ensuring kids don't lose interest? During my first few years of youth ministry, I encountered many parents who thought *I* was responsible. They viewed me as part babysitter, part police officer. They believed a fun and exciting youth program would make their kids want to attend church, and, if their kids didn't want to come to youth activities, it meant there was something wrong with my program.

I quickly learned the value of holding a parents' meeting at least once each year. Parents came with their questions, and together we went through our yearly program. I took time to share the vision I had for the youth group and what I hoped to accomplish in their lives. I always ended the meeting by renewing my commitment to support *their* ministry in the home and expressing my desire to *assist* them in any way possible. That way I reminded them where the primary responsibility lay.

The Bible tells us that parents are responsible for the spiritual development of their children. Churches and youth groups, established for corporate worship, training, and teaching, should reinforce and build on what is already happening in the home. Dean Merrill, in his book, *The Loving Leader: A Man's Role at Home,* puts it this way:

> When we begin to think about our households in the spiritual dimension it's a different story. There is no one to blame but us. There are no church boards or synods standing in the way of progress. If my home reflects the nature and the love of Christ on ordinary Monday, Tuesday, Saturday, it's because my wife and I have determined to make it so. If the atmosphere at our household is no different from that of a non-Christian household, I cannot pass the buck to anyone else.[1]

At home we build the foundation for the spiritual lives of our children. It is the place where attitudes toward church, either positive or negative, are formed. Nothing can take the place of parental example for spiritual training in the home.

WHY DO KIDS LOSE INTEREST IN CHURCH?

A few years ago I had lunch with the father of one of our youth group members at his downtown office. His son was extremely busy in school, held a part-time job, and also maintained an active social life, but was starting to make excuses for not going to youth night at church. I expected him to criticize me or my program, but he surprised me. Instead, he said he recognized his son's spiritual training was his responsibility. He asked if I had any insight into why certain kids become disinterested in spiritual matters. As we talked I shared some of the factors I believe contribute to a child or adolescent not wanting to be involved in the church:

Challenge Authority. One reason kids lose interest in church is because adolescence is a time when many teens challenge the authority of parents, teachers, pastors, and even God. Young people are anxious to grow up and be independent of adult control.

Question Relevancy. Some kids lose interest in church because it no longer seems interesting or relevant. Our children are growing up in a society that competes for their attention through television, movies, and music. As parents and church leaders, we need to offer alternatives, but above all, make them understand their need for Christ and the importance of being part of the body.

Haven't Personalized their Faith. Many individuals come to Christ either through revival or personal difficulty, whose lives are radically changed. But many children born into the homes of such converts haven't personally experienced a dramatic conversion and merely follow the *ethic* of their parents' faith. Young people who grow up in Christian families have a rich heritage, and there are many opportunities for spiritual training and education in a Christian home. Nevertheless, they may become disinterested in the church if they don't *personalize* their faith. It's been said God has no grandchildren, only daughters and sons. We must teach our kids that they can't make it to heaven on our relationship with Christ; we must lead them to a relationship of their own.

Double Standard in the Home. A few years ago, while speaking at a summer camp, I talked with a fifteen-year-old girl who had trouble understanding something her mother had done, and it was interfering with her ability to make a decision for Christ. She said she'd been raised according to the Bible, and her mother, a single parent, had faithfully taken her to church. But she cried as she related that while she was at camp, her mother was in Hawaii with her boyfriend. It was difficult to talk to her about the importance of chastity with the lump in my throat.

It's not enough that we speak the truth to our children; we must live it in front of them. Teens whose parents are not Christians and don't attend church can successfully serve the Lord; teens whose parents are Christians and who are raised in church have an even greater chance of successfully serving the Lord. But teens whose parents live a double standard will rarely decide to follow Christ.

A friend of mine involved in youth ministry once did an informal study to discover why his youth group was losing so many teenagers. In one year alone they lost thirty percent of the kids. This is what he learned:

- Where *both parents* were faithful and active in church, ninety-one percent of the youth remained in church.
- Where only *one parent* was active and faithful, seventy percent of the youth remained in church.
- Where the parents were only *reasonably active* in church, forty-six percent of the youth remained in church.
- Where the parents attended church *infrequently,* only six percent of the youth remained in church.

That underscores the responsibility we have to our kids.

A BIBLICAL FOUNDATION

There is an excellent blueprint for the spiritual development of the family in Deuteronomy 6:4-9:

> Hear, O Israel: The Lord our God, the Lord is one. Love the Lord your God with all your heart and with all your soul and with all your strength. These commandments that I give you today are to be upon your hearts. Impress them on your children. Talk about them when you sit at home and when you walk along the road, when you lie down and when you get up. Tie them as symbols on your hands and bind them on your foreheads. Write them on the doorframes of your houses and on your gates.

These verses are known as the *Shema* and were foundational to the religious education of Hebrew children. They emphasize the importance of obedience, of practicing God's laws daily. Deuteronomy 6:2 gives the reason God gave these commandments to the people of Israel: ". . . so that you, your children and their children after them may fear the Lord your God as long as you live by keeping all his decrees and commands . . . that you may enjoy life." By obeying these commands, the Israelites would live with a constant awareness of God. In fact, these verses established a pattern and direction for the spiritual dimension of Hebrew families that would be passed down from generation to generation.

The instructions were established within the Israelite culture in 1400 B.C., but strong parallels and applications are relevant to the family today. Here are five applications drawn from these verses to help make church life and spiritual matters a positive experience for our children.

Talk about God's laws when you sit at home. What kind of things do you talk about at home? Football, cars, school work, vacation? There's nothing wrong with these things, but do you talk about spiritual matters as well? Notice, I didn't say the church; I said spiritual matters, the things of God. Talk with your children about Jesus Christ, His attributes and characteristics, including His faithfulness. We're instructed to make spiritual matters a regular part of our family conversation.

Talk about God's law when you walk along the road. Israelites didn't have many options when traveling. They could walk or they could ride a donkey. There were no stereos or CD players to entertain them on the journey. Families talked, sang, told stories, and interacted with one another as they traveled. They had time to share the important things of life. In these fast-paced days, we need to *make* time to talk with our families about things that matter. Riding together in the car can offer quality time. Turn off the stereo and talk.

Talk about God's laws when you lie down and when you get up. Some say, "It's how you start and how you finish that's important. Throughout the day there are many interruptions and distractions that can get us off course. This is also true for young people. At school and when interacting with peers, Christian teens face numerous temptations that challenge their faith, but how they start and finish the day can make a difference. If possible, start the day with family prayer. In the evening, around the dinner table, set aside time for family devotions. Don't let your family's spiritual experience consist only of Sunday mornings at church. Make opportunities each day to teach your children about the things of God.

Tie God's laws as symbols on your hands and bind them on your foreheads. The Israelites of Moses' day wore *phylacteries*, little boxes that contained portions of Scripture. The idea was to keep the Word of God close to their hearts and minds. One way to make spiritual matters a positive experience for kids is to make sure they have a readable Bible. You can find several Bibles on the market written specifically for young people, which make it readable and understandable. If we demonstrate a love for God's Word, they will too.

Write God's law on the doorframes of your houses and on your gates. The Bible isn't telling us to paint our homes with scripture verses. The Israelites attached a *mezuzot*, a small wooden or metal container that contained the written Word of God on the doorframes of their homes. If you visit Israel today, you'll still find them in many places. This verse is saying we should have the Word of God around the house, to be conscious of its presence not only in our homes, but also in our lives. When people come into our homes, do they sense something different? Do our neighbors see us model our faith? Do we witness for Jesus Christ? As we impress the law of God on our children's hearts, we'll lay a strong foundation for church life now and in the future.

PRACTICAL APPLICATIONS

We need to make church life a positive experience for our children. Let me offer three practical suggestions to help keep kids in church:

Help your kids be awake and ready for church on Sunday morning. Some parents let their kids stay up late on Saturday night. Then on Sunday morning they struggle to get the kids out of bed. When the family finally gets to church, the children don't get much out of the experience. (See the story of Eutychus in Acts 20:9.) Is it any wonder why some kids dislike church? Let Friday be stay-up-late-night, with extra television or overnight privileges. Get your kids to bed at a reasonable hour on Saturday so they and, for that matter, you will be rested and alert on Sunday, ready to hear God's Word. Sundays are too important to be given less than our best. We need families that are awake and refreshed.

Be willing to make sacrifices to keep your kids in church. I've heard all sorts of titles given to parents, including taxi driver. I've even seen bumper stickers declaring, "Mom's Taxi." It calls for sacrifice to keep kids in church, especially if you live any distance from the church. It's worth the effort to get our kids to church regularly, for service and for youth activities. Patterns are being established that will last a lifetime. Make sure you help set the *right* ones.

Be faithful to the church and its purpose. While I was growing up, church was always the major focus of our family. I have watched too many kids "visit" our church with their parents and, before I could get to the door to greet them and give them a youth calendar, they were gone. We must center our family on the church and its mission and allow our children to see there is much more to church life than simply attending the Sunday morning worship service.

SHOW, DON'T TELL

There are no quick solutions or easy answers to the challenge of keeping kids in church. It takes hard work and time to build a strong, godly foundation in their lives. Home is the primary place for spiritual training, and parents need to take their God-given responsibility seriously. Allow God's commands to the Israelites to transcend the barriers of time and culture and become part of the fabric of your family. Love God with all your being, obey His commands, and teach your children to love and obey Him.

A young father who had a drinking problem decided to walk to the local pub instead of having alcohol in the home. One night during a snowstorm he trudged down the street only to hear the sound of crunching footsteps behind him. He turned to see his five-year-old son trying to put his little boots in the footprints left by his father. Slightly amused, the father asked his son what he was doing. The young boy replied, "I'm trying to follow in your footsteps." Somberly the father picked up his son and headed for home.[2]

My prayer is that, as Christian parents, we will rise to the challenge and model a consistent, godly life.

The Reverend Glenn R. Embree, a frequent speaker at summer camps and youth retreats, is associate pastor at Broadway Church in Vancouver, British Columbia. He worked for twelve years in the youth ministry at Broadway, his home church, after graduating from college. He has been active in Summer A.I.M. outreach programs serving youth in the province of British Columbia. He and his wife Cheryl have two children, Cynthia and Gregg.

18

The Love Factor
COCO PEREZ

Sociologists, psychologists, psychiatrists, and even Planned Parenthood counselors contend that love is the single most important ingredient in parenting. Love is a powerful agent in any type of relationship. That's one point on which everyone agrees. Nevertheless, it's perhaps the most misunderstood emotion, especially in America. For many, it's been reduced to a symbol rather than something of substance. One U. S. stamp has a heart on it with the words "I love you." A postal clerk said it is one of the most popular designs. I thought to myself, *more symbolism.*

Teenage America is bombarded by this kind of symbolism through music, commercial advertising, and even religion. Yet they aren't finding substance or meaning. This generation of teens needs to know and experience the love of God through Jesus, who can break through the meaningless deception of symbolism. If their homes were reinforced by God's love, their lives would be much different.

We need to return to the basics and learn the true meaning of love, which is represented by God's gift of His Son on the cross. It's difficult to comprehend how the cross could be one of the most popular fashion symbols without its true meaning being understood. How did a great Christian nation lose its understanding of God when the hippie movement, perhaps the strangest subculture in American history, was touched by it?

Christian and non-Christian parents know there's a heavy price to pay for not loving their kids as they should. The terrible effects of dysfunctional love permeate our society. The evening news reports one story of sexual abuse after another. I've looked into the pain-filled eyes of teenage boys and girls whose lives have been devastated by dysfunctional love. They need to experience the love of Jesus to understand what real love is. Without the love of Jesus moving and living within our being, we and the church will not amount to anything more than a religious club, the symbol without the substance. As the apostle Paul said, "If I gave everything I have to poor people, and if I were burned alive for preaching the Gospel but didn't love others, it would be of no value whatever" (1 Corinthians 13:3, TLB). In other words, we can do religious things but if we don't have the supernatural love of God in our lives, we will fail as parents and as a church. Ultimately, our children will suffer.

In Revelation 2:1-7, the apostle John was commanded to write a letter to the leader of the church in Ephesus. After commending the church for its good works, John said, "You have forsaken your first love. Remember the height from which you have fallen! Repent and do the things you did at first. If you do not repent, I will come to you and remove your lampstand from its place" (Revelation 2:4,5).

Could it be we've lost our "first love" for God? That excitement we had when we first felt His hand on our lives? The awe of being in His presence? The first commandment is to "Love the Lord your God with all your heart and with all your soul and with all your strength" (Deuteronomy 6:5).

A BIBLICAL DEFINITION OF LOVE

How does the Bible define love? Dr. Paul E. Paino, author of *Catechism in Doctrine*[1], provides an understanding of the three words for love used in the original Greek of the New Testament:

Eros is the root for "erotic." It relates to physical attraction or infatuation. It's a very weak kind of love and cannot be the basis for a fulfilling, sustained relationship. It is based on the desire for pleasure and seeks selfish goals.

Phileo means "brotherly love." It refers to an emotional bond or friendship. We develop friendships based on common values, circumstances, and goals. The family is the first unit for establishing friendships, and it's normal and right for siblings to be friends. Parents also should be friends with their children as well as being authority figures. The Bible teaches that young men should treat young ladies as sisters and friends rather than romantic conquests. It's also important for Christians to develop friendships with other believers. This is one of the values of a local church.

Agape, the word for godly, selfless love, is translated "charity" in the King James Version of the Bible. It is a love based on giving. Love is the fruit of the Spirit and therefore is not determined by the "worthiness" of the person receiving the love. "Charity never faileth" (1 Corinthians 13:8, KJV). Love is the unselfish response of people caring about the needs of others over the needs of self. "God so loved the world, that He *gave* . . ." (John 3:16, NASB). That will be our natural response when we love with an *agape* love. "Greater love hath no man than this, that a man lay down his life for his friends" (John 15:13, KJV).

There are other Greek words for love, but these three relate to the basic parts of man. *Eros* relates to the flesh, or the physical part of man. *Phileo* relates to the soul. It is the response of emotion, intellect, and personality. *Agape* relates to the spirit. It is only by God's Spirit dwelling in us that our spirit can respond to others with genuine *agape* love.

All of us long for *agape,* or selfless, love. God has put a desire for such love in the heart of man. Our young people need to be exposed to such love to counteract the lies perpetrated by the media. As parents, we should be the channel for *agape* love. Our children need to see such love in us to gain a full appreciation of God's love. Teenagers stand as targets in an unholy world. They have more pressures to deal with than ever before: sex, drugs, crime, peer pressure. Combined, they make for a potentially explosive situation. If they can look to us to relieve some of the pressure rather than adding to it and see the sacrificial, selfless love that only comes from God through His Son Jesus, they'll be better equipped to withstand the onslaught of unrighteousness.

The benefits of modeling *agape* love are countless. We can preach, teach, and do all the "religious" things, but if we lack *agape* love, we won't succeed in transferring our value system to our kids. We must not underestimate the value of unconditional love, the kind of love we receive from God. Galatians 5:6 says, "For in Christ Jesus neither circumcision nor uncircumcision has any value. The only thing that counts is faith expressing itself through love."

DO OUR KIDS COME FIRST?

In a day when the nuclear family has attained a lifestyle of luxury, a new set of difficulties, circumstances, and pressures has developed for the family. Phrases such as "stressed out" and "burnout" have become household words. Unfortunately, what we do *outside the home* has become the priority for sustaining the home, rather than what we do *in the home*.

The time factor. Some parents contend they don't have time to express God's love to their teens. Their time is consumed by activities that don't build the family or contribute to the nurturing of their children. The family rises at different times; they don't eat breakfast together; "Good Morning America" is on the TV while the teenager listens to the radio in the bedroom or bathroom; Mom and Dad contemplate their daily schedule over a cup of Taster's Choice. Soon, they'll all go their separate ways to their separate responsibilities, rejoining one another in eight to ten hours. *Maybe* they'll have a meal together, but then it's off to various activities: meetings, homework, laundry.... On the average, children spend less than an hour of interactive time with their parents on any given day.

An article in *Group* magazine reported what kids long to receive from their parents. They want:

- to be trusted
- to be independent while still answering to parents
- to do things with their family
- to love and be loved
- to know their parents accept them for who they are
- to laugh with their parents

But teens don't want:

- parents who are too busy for them
- a "no" without an explanation
- constant nagging
- parents who don't practice what they preach
- parents who are dishonest and undependable
- parents who never discuss family problems with them[2]

Making the family a priority has become alien to our culture. Pastor Glen Cole of Sacramento, California, in speaking about priorities, said, "God comes first, the family comes second, and the church is third." Simple equation, difficult task. Nothing in life is worth having at the expense of losing our teenagers to the world and, inevitably, to the fiery pit of hell.

Giving our time and our lives to our children is an essential expression of *agape* love. It takes time to build any relationship. The key is to start early, while our children are young, then continue to contribute to the relationship when they are teens.

LOVE AND THE REBELLIOUS CHILD

Rebellion has marked much of the youth culture for several generations. Few would argue that the media—via television, movies, and music—have played a major role in furthering the rebellion. A May 1993 Senate inquiry, of which several top Hollywood producers were present, addressed violence in television and movies. They agreed that violence on the screen needs to be curbed and vowed to work together. Unfortunately, it may come too late for many addicted to violence and steeped in rebellion.

How should a parent deal with rebellion? First, we must recognize some things happen simply because they're teens. All teenagers go through major changes, and those changes often bring about a change in behavior. They vary in intensity based on temperament, social climate, upbringing, and spiritual development. An age-level characteristics chart may help parents understand where their teen is physically and emotionally:

Junior High	Senior High
Puberty begins	Reaches physical maturity
Rapid muscular growth	Searching for ideals
Enormous appetite	Sexual maturity is reached
Tires easily	High interest in philosophical, ethical, and religious problems
Easily frustrated	
Retreats into fantasy world	Forms cliques
Awkward, restless, lazy	Prone to self-pity
Looks for warm affection and humor in adult sponsors	High interest in physical being
Looks for assurances of security[3]	

The differences between junior and senior high are dramatic. Parents who understand these factors will better know how to relate to and pray for their teens.

Second, we must recognize our teens are not the enemy.

A parent commented, "Raising my fifteen-year-old has been real spiritual warfare." Many parents feel that way about raising teenagers. The enemy targets the home and teens in particular. The devil is no fool; he takes advantage of the most tumultuous time in a person's life to draw him away from God. Unfortunately, the teenager stands out as a prime target. In a counseling session, a parent said, "I wish we could pack everything up and leave the house to our (teenage) son." That isn't the answer, and the son isn't the enemy. 1 Peter 5:8 says, ". . . Your enemy the devil prowls around like a roaring lion looking for someone to devour." *Satan* is the enemy, and unless we're on guard, our kids will become his prey.

Rebellion is an evil seed planted in our hearts by Satan. *Agape* love, which hates the sin but loves the sinner, is powerful enough to destroy it. We must look beyond the natural into the spiritual realm where the apostle Paul identifies the source of the problem. "For our struggle is not against flesh and blood, but against the rulers, against the authorities, against the powers of this dark world and against the spiritual forces of evil in the heavenly realms" (Ephesians 6:12). God's love is able to penetrate the darkness of evil. "The weapons we fight with are not the weapons of the world. On the contrary, they have divine power to demolish strongholds" (2 Corinthians 10:4). *Agape* love is just such a weapon, but it's been underestimated by the Christian community. It's what redeemed us from our fallen state; it will do the same for our rebellious teens.

1 Thessalonians 5:18 says, "But since we belong to the day, let us be self-controlled, putting on faith and love as a breastplate, and the hope of salvation as a helmet." This suggests that God's love is not only an offensive weapon, it's a defensive weapon as well, protecting us from the fiery missiles the enemy aims at our hearts. But when is the love of God activated? When we channel His mercy and grace to others in need. We have an advantage over the enemy when we surrender our *feelings* and respond to our teens in Christian love.

SPARE THE ROD

If we love our children, we will discipline them. Parents who do not have a consistent, loving, biblical approach to discipline do not have their children's well-being at heart. This includes corporal punishment. Despite what secularists believe, the Bible is the final authority in determining truth for the Christian. This is what the Bible has to say about love and discipline:

> He who spares the rod hates his son, but he who loves him is careful to discipline him—Proverbs 13:24.
>
> Folly is bound up in the heart of a child, but the rod of discipline will drive it far from him—Proverbs 22:15.
>
> Do not withhold discipline from a child; if you punish him with the rod, he will not die—Proverbs 23:13.

The Word of God makes it clear that parents who love their children will discipline them.

If your home lacks *agape* love, go to the Source. God has an unlimited supply and desires to pour it out on His children.

Coco Perez graduated from Berean College with a major in Ministerial Studies. He is A.I.M. director for the Northern California/Nevada district of the Assemblies of God, which trains and equips young people for missionary work. He is also an evangelist based out of Capital Christian Center in Sacramento, California.

The Reverend Perez spent twelve years as a youth pastor and has been a camp speaker and seminar teacher on parenting. He has served on the boards of Teen Challenge and Youth for Christ.

He and his wife Lynn have two children: Jarus and Zachariah.

19

Kids 'In Christ'

KEVIN NEWTON

The morning began with little difficulty for the father of a newborn. It was the first time he'd been left in charge of his baby boy. After a successful bath, the father's confidence soared. Breakfast was no problem since formula was the only item on the menu. Everything was going smoothly . . . until 10:30, when the first sign of trouble appeared. Baby Boy was growing noticeably uncomfortable while Dad raced for rattles and a stuffed raccoon for a diversion. Panic set in by 11:00, for nothing would calm the child who had healthy lungs and a resolve to use them.

Even so, the proud father couldn't bring himself to phone Mom for advice. Admitting defeat wasn't on his favorite-things-to-do list. But soliciting help from Grandma was a different thing altogether. Within minutes, the parenting pro arrived to rescue her son. It took only seconds to assess the problem.

"When was he last changed?" she asked, wrinkling her nose.

"Changed? You mean . . ." (he pointed to the diaper) "changed? Well, gee, I uh . . . How often do you have to do that?"

"That's up to him," Grandma said, smiling at her grandchild.

In no time Baby Boy was clean, dry, and happy.

Babies don't come with instructions, but parents aren't without hope. God has given us the Bible, and it's filled with instructions for good parenting, including teaching our children who they are in Christ. But it's not enough to *read* the directions of the Bible; we must *understand* them as well. A great service we can provide our children is to give quality answers to the questions they ask, especially when they concern their walk with Christ: how they become a Christian, how they stay a Christian, and what God wants from them.

TAKE RESPONSIBILITY

Today's youth are growing up in a complex society with pressures that previous generations did not have to face. The media through television, movies, and music has a tremendous influence on this generation of young people. Parents must not abdicate their position, willingly or unwillingly. We cannot be responsible for an entire generation, but we must be responsible for our own children. If that means fighting off the world's influence to make our own effective, then we'd better roll up our sleeves and prepare for battle.

Parents who really "parent," who spend time and energy on their children, are becoming a rare breed. Too often parents look to teachers and youth pastors to instruct and influence their children. While other adults can provide healthy role models, the responsibility unquestionably lies with parents.

This chapter will discuss who we are in Christ and will equip us to teach our children who they are in Christ, providing a foundation that will stay with them for the rest of their lives. They need to understand who they are in Christ, what God wants from them, and how they can approach Him. Such knowledge will make them less susceptible to worldly influences and more stable in their Christian walk.

BUILDING THE FOUNDATION

Three passages of Scripture provide a foundation for Christian living. The first is Ephesians 2:1-6:

Alive in Christ.
> And you were dead in your trespasses and sins, in which you formerly walked according to the course of this world, according to the prince of the power of the air, of the spirit that is now working in the sons of disobedience. Among them we too all formerly lived in the lusts of our flesh, indulging the desires of the flesh and of the mind, and were by nature children of wrath, even as the rest. But God, being rich in mercy, because of His great love with which He loved us, even when we were dead in our transgressions, made us alive together with Christ (by grace you have been saved), and raised us up with Him, and seated us with Him in the heavenly places, in Christ Jesus (NASB).

This passage is not so much a theological message on the benefits of our salvation as it is an expression of the apostle

Paul's heart, which is overwhelmed with the indescribable grace and mercy of the God who saved him. In the original Greek this passage is marked with bad grammar, incomplete sentences, and mid-sentence construction change; verses one through seven are all one sentence. It's obvious Paul was pouring out his heart; the rules of grammar were unimportant.

Verses one to three leave no mistake that in our fallen state it was impossible for us to have a relationship with God. We were dead in sin, walking in accordance with the world, living in partnership with the prince of the air, and disobedient. We needed help from a source beyond ourselves. God provided it in three ways:

First, though we were dead in sin, He kept us alive.

Sadly, it's not uncommon to hear Christians talk about serving God with words that make it sound like they're doing Him a favor. They forget that God is our very Source of life. He doesn't *have* to be; He *chooses* to be.

Second, even before we were believers, God raised us up with Christ: brought us up to heavenly places, with access to the very throne of God. It was not in our power to ascend to Him; He made it possible. To illustrate, several years ago I was the first to arrive at the scene of a head-on collision between a truck and a small car. The engine of the automobile had been pushed into the driver's lap, trapping him in his vehicle. He was absolutely helpless to free himself. We were equally trapped in a dimension that cannot reach God. It's absurdly prideful to think we've done anything to attain the heights to which God has raised us.

Third, while we were yet sinners God seated us with Christ in heavenly places, complete in Jesus. God isn't bound by time; He knows the score before the end of the game, or as Isaiah 46:9,10 says: "I am God, and there is none like Me, declaring the end from the beginning, and ... things that are not yet done ..." (NKJV).

So God sees us *alive* with Christ, *raised up* with Christ, and *seated* with Christ in heavenly places, all because of faith. The amazing thing is that God even gives us the faith to believe unto salvation.

Many young people in our churches really don't know how God views them. They're often presented with a gospel that's more of a to-do list than a free gift, and they fall into a routine of performing for God's approval. The problem is compounded by another list of how Christians should *look,* which produces the feeling that they'll never match up to God's standard. But God's Word teaches us the truth: by faith we receive what God has done for us. And that truth will set them and us free to enjoy an abundant relationship that God initiated.

Guard Our Hearts. Hebrews 3:12-14 is another key passage that will help our children understand the Christian life. A common question among youth is: "What does God want from me?" It may or may not be verbally expressed, but it's both real and revealing. They need to understand that God is concerned with what they watch on television and what music they listen to, but it's secondary to what has taken place in the heart. It always goes back to works versus faith. If our teens feel they are Christians based on what they *do,* or how they *perform,* that their behavior validates their relationship with Christ, they've missed the heart of the gospel. And that could cause them to walk away from God with the feeling they'll never measure up, so why bother? The truth is, they *won't* measure up and neither will we. The author of Hebrews made sure that we understand what God wants from us.

Every parent goes through the memorable experience of potty training their children. I certainly remember when my wife and I reached that phase of parenting.

We began by explaining the fundamental principles of the bathroom to our daughter, introducing her to the various bathroom fixtures, eager to be free from the tyranny of diapers. No more runs to the Quick Stop at midnight where we'd spend $73.95 for sixteen diapers.

We imagined the fresh clean mountain air that would sweep down from the range and into our home without being tainted by the little, white diaper pail in the corner of the room. With this to spur us on, we diligently explained what the toilet was for and how it is used. Certain of imminent success, we watched as our daughter marched into her bedroom, scooped up her very favorite stuffed Sesame Street character Elmo (for moral support, of course), made her way to the bathroom, and dropped him into the toilet. She proudly proclaimed, "Elmo go potty." We suspected then that potty training was far from over.

Our daughter had missed the point, but Hebrews 3:12-14 makes it clear what God wants from us so we don't. It says:

> Take care, brethren, lest there should be in any one of you an evil, unbelieving heart, in falling away from the living God. But encourage one another day after day, as long as it is still called "Today," lest any one of you be hardened by the deceitfulness of sin. For we have become partakers of Christ, if we hold fast the beginning of our assurance firm until the end (NASB).

We're admonished here to "take care" lest there be a wicked, unbelieving heart in us. We must guard our hearts and protect the faith that we possess and encourage and teach our children to guard their hearts as well.

The Amplified version puts it this way: ". . . take care lest there be in any one of you a wicked, unbelieving heart—which refuses to cleave to, trust in and rely on Him" (Hebrews 3:12). Notice the author did not say an unbelieving *mind*. There's a big difference. The mind is where we reason; the heart is where we believe.

It's said of the Bereans in Acts 17:11, "Now these were more noble-minded than those in Thessalonica, for they received the word with great eagerness, examining the Scriptures daily, to see whether these things were so" (NASB). The noble Bereans were not arrogant or prideful; they were discerning and discriminatory in what they believed.

When our children ask questions about God, we can't toss out answers such as, "That's just what we believe" or "That's what the church teaches." We have a God-given need for answers to life's questions; so do our children. Don't be afraid that their questions indicate unbelief. They have legitimate questions that need a response. One of the greatest gifts we can give is the freedom to question and seek answers that satisfy. This will give them the opportunity to say: "Christianity is not just my parents' belief or my church's belief; it is my belief."

Hebrews 3:14 in the Amplified Bible says, "For we have become fellows with Christ, the Messiah, and share in all He has for us, if only we hold our first newborn confidence and original assured expectation [in virtue of which we are believers] firm and unshaken to the end."

Hebrews 3:15 quotes Psalm 95 concerning the people of Israel at Kadesh, after they were led out of Egypt and into the wilderness, where they contemplated electing a new leader and returning to Egypt. The author draws a parallel between those who reject salvation by grace through Jesus Christ and those who wanted to return to Egypt. Both groups rejected the process of pilgrimage. They were unwilling to be a people of faith, afraid to learn what life in Jesus is all about.

But Hebrews 3:14 says we have become *fellows* with Christ. For that reason we must not turn back to the Law, which could only show us our sin, not save us from it. The Lane translation says, "We have become fellows with Christ, supposing that we hold firmly to the end the basic position we had at the beginning."[1] What is the basic position of Christian faith? Through faith in Jesus, our sins are forgiven; Jesus lives in and through us, and our ambition is to follow Christ. Through faith we understand salvation is a gift from God; it would be futile to return to our old life or the law for righteousness. The Hebrews lost sight of each point. It's up to us to make sure we and our children "hold firmly to the end the basic position we had at the beginning."

As a boy, I learned the premise of Hebrews 3:12-14. I started out well, full of joy, peace, and new life. I got involved in the church and started to grow in my faith. But message after message, teaching after teaching, impressed upon me that if I was really saved and really spiritual, my life would show it in a particular way. As a result, I began to feel I could never meet God's standards and spent a great deal of time dealing with sin and guilt. I was preoccupied with *being* right before God, while failing to *feel* right before Him. I doubted that Jesus could live in and through me while I was in such a sinful state so much of the time. I relieved my guilt by serving God in any capacity I could find, in and out of the church. Salvation began to feel like something I earned instead of a free gift from God.

The U. S. Army slogan is: "It's not just a job; its an adventure." I began to feel that Christian life was not just an adventure; it was a job. The list of things I had to do to earn God's favor had gotten too long. Preachers continually reinforced from the pulpit that God was primarily concerned with what I watched on television, what radio station I listened to, and what movies I saw. I lost my ambition to serve Christ, along with the joy, peace, and freedom I'd found in Him, and returned to legalism to appease an angry God I could never approach. I was not holding on to the basic position of a believer, and Christianity was more of a burden than a blessing. Fortunately, God restored me to the place of faith where I'd begun my walk.

Our children will fall into the same trap unless we help them understand the basic position of their faith in Christ, taught in Hebrews 3:12-14. Well-meaning individuals can make Christianity so difficult we cannot succeed; Christ meant for faith to be so simple we could not fail. If we model for our children that we're accepted by God because of His grace, and we serve Him because of our love, they'll follow the example we set.

Draw Near. The final key passage of Scripture we'll discuss in this chapter is tied to how we approach God. If I were to ask, "On what basis do you have a relationship with God?" what would you say? Hebrews 4:14-16 makes it clear there's only *one* correct answer: through Christ.

> Since then we have a great high priest who has passed through the heavens, Jesus the Son of God, let us hold fast our confession. For we do not have a high priest who cannot sympathize with our weaknesses, but one who has been tempted in all things as we are, yet without sin. Let us therefore

draw near with confidence to the throne of grace, that we may receive mercy and may find grace to help in time of need (NASB).

As a youth evangelist I was continually approached by teens who expressed their frustration at not feeling "right" enough to approach God. I explained that we do not approach God based on our goodness, but on our faith in Christ's righteousness. They usually responded with confusion or disbelief, having never heard that before. They'd been raised in the understanding that you had to have your act together for God to like you.

Hebrews 4:14-16 will help us explain to our children that if our ambition is to follow Christ, even if we make mistakes we are no less accepted by God. If they understand that their access to God is not threatened by mistakes, they won't be frustrated at their inability to be "right enough" to approach Him.

The author of Hebrews gives four reasons why we can confidently approach God through Christ. First, because Jesus is our High Priest. That was a tremendous revelation for the early readers of Hebrews who had always depended on the Levitical high priest to be the mediator between them and God; without him, there was no access to Jehovah. The high priest could approach God's throne only once a year, but with Christ as high priest, God's people have access to Him at any time.

Second, we can approach God through Jesus because He has ascended to the right hand of the Father where He intercedes for us. He established a new covenant in His own blood that was able to remove all sin.

Third, we can approach God because Jesus is not merely a good man or a great teacher: He is the Son of God. We've become familiar with this title, but to the infant church it was a new and remarkable revelation, one in which they took courage and comfort.

Finally, we have confidence in approaching God because Jesus can empathize with our temptations and weaknesses. He experienced our frailties and was tempted in every way we are today, yet without sin. Jesus knows all about us and still chooses to serve as our high priest before God. He identifies with our sin, yet is sinless; therefore He is worthy and able to cover us.

I accompanied the Oakland A's chaplain to chapel one Sunday morning. We drove to the stadium two hours before the day's game started and entered the players' parking lot where a security guard checked our pass. After parking we walked into the players' entrance amidst heavy security. As we passed through various security points the chaplain would say, "He's with me," and I was admitted. Had I not been with the chaplain, I never would have gotten past the parking lot. I could have explained how much I loved baseball and how far I could hit the ball, but it would have meant nothing had I not been with the right person.

That's what Jesus says when we go before God's throne. He says, "Father, they're with me." Based on our ability, our talent, our good works? Of course not. We approach God based on our faith in Jesus Christ.

The reasons we can approach the throne of grace with confidence have nothing to do with *our* worthiness; they're all based on *Christ's* worthiness. Yet failure keeps us from approaching God when we need to the most. Can we approach Him with any more confidence when we're at our best? Let's not fool ourselves. Our best is filthy rags. Hebrews 4:16 tells us to approach the throne of grace with confidence because of our position in Christ so that we may find mercy and grace in time of need.

As we instruct our children in the ways of God, we'll save them years of frustration and disappointment if we help them understand who they are in Christ, what God wants from them, and how they can approach God. We must not leave this instruction to others; it's our responsibility. When they come with questions we'll serve them best by having answers.

The Reverend Kevin Newton is singles pastor at Lakeview Assembly in Stockton, California. He pioneered Impact Team, a crusade evangelism team that has ministered in hundreds of public school assemblies and evangelistic rallies. He also developed Higher Ground Singles Ministry. Kevin has authored two ministry manuals: Lay Pastor and Net Group Training Manual *and* Divorce Recovery Manual. *He received his B. A. from Bethany Bible College and is currently enrolled at Fuller Theological Seminary in the Master of Theology Program. He and his wife Becky have a two-year-old daughter, Arielle.*

20

God in the Public School

JAMES 'RAT' SAUNDERS

As a youth pastor drove onto a public school campus to speak at an assembly, he noticed the principal standing at the front door to meet him. He welcomed him with open arms and said how excited he was to have him there, but he did have one thing to say before the assembly. *This is where I get the lecture about mixing church and state,* the youth pastor said to himself. Instead, the principal said, "When you're finished with the assembly I want you to ask all 1,200 students to invite Jesus Christ into their lives." Needless to say, the youth pastor was amazed. And when he finished his presentation, he did just what the principal had asked. He gave an altar call, and over three-fourths of the student body came forward and made a decision for Christ.[1]

You may be thinking, that's great but it's also illegal. You're right. It's illegal to give an altar call in a public school in the United States. But this story took place in

Russia, a country that rejected the gospel for decades but is now hungry for the Word of God.

The myth of separation of church and state has been used as grounds to expel God from the public school system. But Christians still have rights guaranteed by the Constitution. We need to learn what they are and exercise them.

THE PUBLIC SCHOOL AS A MISSION FIELD

Who would you say has the largest youth group in your area? The Baptists? The Nazarenes? The Assemblies of God? No, the largest youth group anywhere is found on junior high and high school campuses. The church has put great efforts into missions, and rightly so, but we need to reach our "Jerusalem" as well. The public schools in our area are a huge mission field that we often overlook.

We live in a country where religious freedom is just that—the right to freely express one's religious beliefs. No matter how it may appear, the courts are on our side. In 1984, Congress ruled schools could not discriminate against public school students because of their religious beliefs.[2] On June 4, 1990, the U. S. Supreme Court upheld the ruling. It said public secondary schools receiving federal funds and allowing non-curriculum related clubs to meet on campus must also allow Bible clubs and prayer groups, as long as they're initiated by students. The Equal Access Act of 1984 also provides that guest speakers may be invited to speak in Christian clubs.

Contrary to popular belief, the courts haven't entirely disallowed prayer at school graduations; they ruled prayer is permissible when it's a voluntary, student-led prayer. Student speakers, such as a valedictorian or salutatorian, may initiate prayers, give Christian testimonies, and acknowledge God as they choose. As Acts 4:29 states: "And now, Lord ... grant that Thy bond-servants may speak Thy Word with all confidence ..." (NASB).

PRAYER AND THE PUBLIC SCHOOL

Because the public school system has such an influence on our children, we cannot allow the enemy to gain any more ground. We must exercise our rights and take back what belongs to us. Many of the efforts made against Christians look too big to combat, but we serve a great God. We need revival in our public schools, and prayer can make it happen. Consider the following: Farmer Johnson went into a hardware store where he was told a new chainsaw could cut five large oak trees in an hour. He bought the chainsaw and went to work. Before long, he was mad. The new saw only cut one tree in eight hours. When he took it back to the hardware store, the surprised owner took the saw outside and pulled the cord. A bewildered Farmer Johnson asked, "What's that noise?" Many today make the same mistake by trying to accomplish spiritual feats on their own power. We need God's power, and that power comes through prayer. We've made inroads regarding Christian rights in the public arena, but we have a long way to go. Prayer must accompany action as we persevere.

RELIGIOUS RIGHTS

The U. S. Supreme Court has ruled that a school may not impose religious instruction or mandatory prayer upon its students, but it hasn't prohibited these activities altogether. Students have constitutionally protected rights that are not surrendered when they walk onto campus. The *Students'*

Bill of Rights on a Public School Campus[3] will help you and your child understand the law. Here are its points:

The right to meet with other religious students. Students have the right to meet anywhere on campus to discuss religious issues. Students may share their religious beliefs with any other student. They cannot force their beliefs on others, nor can they disrupt school activities, but students are otherwise able to exercise their religious freedoms.

One afternoon I went to a high school to speak at a Bible club. The principal, who wasn't familiar with the Students' Bill of Rights, asked what I planned to do at the meeting. I told him as part of my visit I planned to read the Bible and pray. He nervously said he didn't believe I was permitted to do either activity. Like many principals, he was misinformed. I said I would respect his wishes and not read the Bible or pray, but I promised to bring him a copy of the *Students' Bill of Rights.* Some would have argued, knowing the law protected their rights, but I didn't want to jeopardize my relationship with the principal or the Bible club. I told the members that I was asked not to pray or read the Bible, but since I wasn't asked not to quote Scripture from memory, that's what I did. That day, more than sixty students gave their lives to Jesus Christ. Now, more than two hundred students attend that Bible club, and they've impacted their school and their community.[4]

The right to identify religious beliefs through signs and symbols. Students are allowed to wear clothing and jewelry that display religious sayings and symbols. They're also allowed to have Christian book covers and to hang posters in their lockers. These can be great witnessing tools. As a further witness, Christian students could select a day to wear t-shirts or sweat shirts that lift up the name of Christ.

The right to talk about religious beliefs on campus. Students are permitted to talk individually or in groups about religious issues, including inviting other students to go to church with them. They can share subjects discussed in church or youth group. They might consider using the following survey as a tool to reach fellow students:

1. Do you attend church?   [ ] yes   [ ] no
2. Do you attend a youth group? [ ] yes   [ ] no
3. Do you believe in heaven?   [ ] yes   [ ] no
4. Do you believe in hell?   [ ] yes   [ ] no
5. Where do you think you'll go when you die?

After sharing the survey, students can invite other students to attend church with them or even lead them in a sinner's prayer.

The right to distribute religious literature on campus. Students may hand out tracts, flyers, or other religious materials on campus. They may not distribute them during class time, nor can they stuff them into lockers. They must individually hand such materials to another student. Christian clubs have the right to use school bulletin boards and the public address system for advertising purposes, as long as other campus clubs are permitted to do the same.

The right to pray on campus. Students are allowed to pray over their meals and with other students, as long as they don't disrupt the activities of others.

The right to carry or study the Bible on campus. Students may take their Bibles to school and read them during study times or after tests while waiting for other students to finish.

At a local high school, a student was dismissed from the classroom for reading his Bible after a test. The assistant principal supported the teacher's actions. When I contacted them, I found they didn't know the student was within his rights.

The right to do research papers, speeches, and creative projects with religious themes. Students have the right to do research papers on biblical themes, to talk or write about the Bible in literature and history classes, and to do presentations and art projects on religious subjects. Giving a personal testimony during a speech or addressing subjects such as Christian values, abortion, and cults are well within a student's rights.

The right to be exempt. Parents have the right to review materials taught in the classroom and, when they violate religious beliefs, request alternate materials. Students can be exempt from participating in class assignments that are contrary to religious beliefs. A proper chain of command should be used when requesting alternate assignments, beginning with the teacher. If the teacher will not grant the request, go to the principal. If that doesn't work, go to the superintendent. Next, contact your school board, and if you haven't been satisfied, take the matter to court. Usually, the teacher or principal will comply with a parent's or student's request.

Christian children should not be force-fed ideals that go against God's principles. For example, they should not be forced to color witches and other occult symbols during Halloween. Parents are well within their rights to have their children exempted from such assignments or activities. It's important for parents to preview materials for sex education, AIDS awareness, and other controversial health issues.

Know what's being taught and, when it violates your religious beliefs, exercise your rights.

The right to celebrate and study religious holidays on campus. Students can distribute Christmas cards, sing religious carols, and study the meaning of Easter, Christmas, and other religious holidays.

The right to meet with school officials. The school board is your friend. Many board members run for office because they care about young people. Generally, they will listen when you attend meetings to discuss issues that affect your children. If you feel your child is being treated unfairly on religious issues, go to the board and voice your concerns. If they are unwilling to listen, elect school board members that will be sensitive to such issues.

There are excellent materials that can help Christian students make a stand on their public campuses. *Take a Stand,* a campus ministry manual for students, produced by the Youth Alive Department of the Assemblies of God, is one.[5]

For Christians, the public school campus is the major battleground of the free speech issue. Our young people must not be deceived into silence. Eight-five percent of those who come to Christ do so before they graduate from high school. With so many life and death issues facing teens today, they need to know about Christ. Christian students are the only ones that can reach them on campus. As Jeff Swain, Youth Alive director of the Assemblies of God, says, "You're either a missionary or a mission field."

Parents, you don't have the same rights on campus as your children, but you *can* get involved. Pray for teachers, administrators, staff, and school board members. Volunteer in your children's classrooms. Get involved in PTA. Be a presence in the public school system, and be a silent but positive witness for Christ.

If you experience problems concerning religious rights on campus, contact one of the following organizations for assistance:

National Legal Foundation
6477 College Park Square, Ste. 306
Virginia Beach, VA 23464
(804) 424-4242

C.A.S.E.
(Christian Advocates Serving Evangelism)
P.O. Box 450349
Atlanta, GA 30345
(804) 523-7239

For more information about student rights on campus, purchase "Students' Legal Rights" by J. W. Brinkley.[6]

The Reverend James "Rat" Saunders has served as youth pastor at Trinity Assembly of God in Fairmont, West Virginia for six years. He is a popular speaker at youth camps, conventions, revivals, and in junior high and high school assemblies. He has also served on the Marion County Board of Education for the past ten years. He has organized Bible clubs in West Virginia, Pennsylvania, Virginia, Maryland, and Washington, D. C. and holds seminars on students legal rights.

He graduated from Southeastern External Degree Program College with a major in Bible and Theology.

He and his wife Pam are the parents of eighteen-year-old Jason and seventeen-year-old Jaime.

CHARACTER DEVELOPMENT

*Until youth learn to know, respect, and obey
the teachings of Almighty God, we can never expect them
to obey civil law or the laws of society.*

Anonymous

21

The Power of Encouragement

BILLY WILLIAMS

I'll never forget Mrs. Piner, my third grade teacher. She wore bright red lipstick, pink blush, and glasses so clean I could see myself in them. She never raised her voice, and her words were always kind. She had a way of making each one of her students feel important. What a lady!

Do you recall the little styrofoam cup that everyone had in the third grade? You know, the one the whole class took out to the play yard with them to find dirt (that wasn't there). You had to fill your cup with sand that came from under the swing-set. After we returned to class, Mrs. Piner gave us all a bean to plant. Even though we planted the beans at the same time, we didn't see similar results. I swore some of my classmates had magical beans, because the next day we came to school and they seemed to reach the ceiling. All of them, except mine.

Mrs. Piner reassured me that mine would grow. I knew someone had snuck into the class in the middle of the night and stole the bean right out of my cup. She assured me it wasn't so. I believed her and waited patiently. Well, the day came when my bean began to sprout. I was ecstatic—and Mrs. Piner was thrilled, too. She continued to encourage me as we both watched this plant grow. Little did I know that at the same time she was watching the bean grow, she was watching me grow as well. From the inside out.

Mrs. Piner always cheered me on, even when the other students had other things to say to me. I never had another teacher like her in grade school. I give her an A. An A for never giving up and for always looking for the growth in me—even when she couldn't see it. It's kind of like some of us. God has planted a seed of potential in each one of us. Sometimes it just takes a little longer to sprout. But then, there are the Mrs. Piners in our lives who, through constant encouragement, through kind words, build up what is not yet seen. Everyone needs a Mrs. Piner.

WORDS BUILD OR DESTROY

We sometimes forget what power is in the tongue. Our words can build up or they can tear down; they can heal or they can destroy. I discovered many years ago I have to be careful what I say to my family and how I say it. Words can be harmless in themselves, but the way we use them can be destructive. This chapter will give helpful insight on how to encourage those around us, with special emphasis on our children.

The art of encouragement must be cultivated. We must make a conscious effort to be encouragers if we're to make a positive difference in other people's lives, striving for a spirit of encouragement especially in our homes. When we achieve that, there will be a spirit of unity as well. Encouragement and unity go hand in hand. Romans 15:5 says, "May the God who gives endurance and encouragement give you a spirit of unity among yourselves as you follow Christ Jesus . . ."

The apostle Paul knew the Ephesians loved Jesus. The purpose of his letter was to strengthen them in their Christian faith. He penned a verse that we should live by today: "Do not let any unwholesome talk come out of your mouths, but only what is helpful for building others up according to their needs, that it may benefit those who listen" (Ephesians 4:29). The Living Bible says it another way: "Don't use bad language. Say only what is good and helpful to those you are talking to, and what will give them a blessing." The Beck Translation says: "Don't say anything bad but only what is good, so that you help where there's a need and benefit those who hear it."

Encouraging others needs to be at the very center of our lifestyle. The Greek word for "edify" is *oikodome*; it denotes the act of building others to make them strong. Do our words build others? Do they make others strong? Do we speak edifying words every day? It's never too late to start cultivating this art.

- E   Be an Example
- N   Don't Nag
- C   Challenge to Excellence
- O   Be an Overcomer
- U   When there is Unity
- R   Resist Revenge
- A   Appreciate People/Have an Attitude of Gratitude
- G   Give a Gift
- E   Encourage, Encourage, Encourage

BE AN EXAMPLE

To be an encourager, we must first be an example. In the apostle Paul's writing to young Titus, he urged him to be a good example so others might see his good deeds and imitate him. His life would give his words greater impact. If we want our children to act a certain way, we have to live that way ourselves. Think of a person who has influenced your life. Were you influenced by what they said or by what they did? Talk is cheap. Our actions must always back up our words. Many parents assume their kids will do what they say, when most will emulate what they do.

One afternoon a young girl dropped in at my office. I could tell her spirits were down. She could hardly look me in the eyes. I asked her what was wrong. It took only a few minutes for her to begin to share. "I just got suspended from school for three days," she said. She looked up, and with tears falling down her cheeks, said, "I was caught drinking at school." She had drunk some vodka and some peppermint schnapps. "Where did you get the stuff?" I asked. Her answer was one that I have heard many times. "I got it at my house. It was in my mom's kitchen." Do you think her mother approved of her junior high girl getting suspended from school for drinking? Absolutely not. But her parents really set the stage by their example at home. The girl had been watching her parents drink and wanted to try it herself. To be an encourager, we must set the example for our kids in deeds and words.

Today start setting an example of encouraging those closest to you—your family. We often overlook the most important people to us. Use your words to build up. Stop the negative talk. Stop the bad language. When you use words that build others up, it really benefits everyone who hears what you say. When you give someone a word of support, a kind word, it builds them up. You and I would have people running to our door if only we could learn the art of encouraging.

DON'T NAG

As parents, we often have to stay on top of our kids when it comes to responsibilities around the house. Getting them to clean their room, take out the garbage, do the dishes, or whatever their chores may be, may be a chore in itself to see them follow through. It's easy to fall into a habit of nagging. When we nag we become negative, and when we become negative our tongue usually gets the best of us. "A constant dripping on a rainy day and a cranky woman are much alike. You can no more stop her complaints than you can stop the wind or hold onto anything with oil-slick hands" (Proverbs 27:15,16, TLB).

There are ways to accomplish what we want without nagging, which seldom accomplishes anything. When we're tempted to nag, we need to restrain ourselves and try to persuade instead. The word "persuasion" is derived from two Latin terms: *per* meaning "through" and *suasio* meaning "sweetness." It literally means "moving people through sweetness." We'd accomplish more and discourage less if we took the time to persuade rather than nag.

James 3:2 says, "If anyone can control his tongue, it proves that he has perfect control over himself in every other way" (TLB), and self-control is a fruit of the Spirit. When we yield our speech to God, our words will be full of mercy, love, peace, courtesy, sincerity, gentleness, and goodness, all aspects of being an encourager.

CHALLENGE TO EXCELLENCE

Ask a successful person what has helped them get where they are in life, and invariably they'll talk about a goal, a dream, a mission—something bigger than they are. Young people today need to be challenged out of their comfort zone; to believe in something bigger than themselves. We need to encourage them to dream big dreams, but we'll never accomplish the task unless we are motivated. We'll never stir our kids beyond mediocrity if we haven't been stirred beyond it ourselves.

The same applies to the spiritual realm. Our kids need to see us hunger and thirst for a deeper presence of God in our lives. We need to be passionate for the Lord if we expect them to be. We need to encourage our kids to walk close to Him, to rely on Him for every need, to live a life pleasing to Him by our words and our deeds.

Proverbs 29:18 says, "Where there is no vision [dream], the people perish" (KJV). Heavenly visions allow us to see our position, potential, and possibility in Christ. They encourage us to give up all that we are in order to receive all we can become. Young people need to be challenged to live a life of excellence before the Lord. Our encouragement may be the driving force they need to start them on their way.

BE AN OVERCOMER

"They overcame him by the blood of the Lamb and by the word of their testimony" (Revelation 12:11). When life's obstacles trip us on our journey, we cannot stay down; we cannot be defeated. We must let our kids see the power of God operating in our lives. The way they see us respond to life's trials is the way they will respond to the trials that come their way. Ask yourself this question: Do I *react* to problems, or do I *respond* to them? We must make a concerted effort to have an overcomer's attitude every minute of every day. The following five points will help us accomplish that:

1. I refuse to be shackled by yesterday's failures.
2. What I don't know will no longer be an intimidation; it will be an opportunity.
3. I will not allow people to define my mood, my method, my image, or my mission.
4. I will pursue a mission greater than myself by making at least one person glad that they saw me today.
5. I will have no time for self-pity, gossip, or negativism . . . for myself or others.

I can do everything through him who gives me strength (Philippians 4:13). I will be an overcomer.

WHEN THERE IS UNITY

"All the believers were together and had everything in common" (Acts 2:44). What would happen if there was that kind of unity in every family and in every church? The time we'd gain by not fighting each other could be spent on defeating the enemy of our souls.

Through the years I've been on some great camping adventures with young people. I enjoy observing teens from diverse ethnic groups and socio-economic backgrounds coming together in the name of the Lord. When unity takes over, differences disappear and, as in the early church, they have all things in common.

Unfortunately, many young people don't experience unity, even in their own homes. Instead, many try to play peacemaker between feuding parents while others wish they could get along with family members. Psalm 133:1 says, "How good and pleasant it is when brothers live together in unity!" Ephesians 4:3 adds, "Make every effort to keep the unity of the Spirit through the bond of peace."

Here are some thoughts for cultivating unity at home:

1. Create an atmosphere of acceptance. Be quick to listen, slow to speak, slow to become angry, and let them talk.
2. Renew your devotion to each other.
3. Eat together, pray together, and have fun together.
4. Learn to laugh together. Stop taking life so seriously.

RESIST REVENGE

If we want to teach our kids to be encouragers, we must teach them to resist revenge. It's our nature to want to retaliate when evil comes our way, but when we're in Christ we are new creatures (see 2 Corinthians 5:17) and don't have to give in to the old nature. We are admonished to do good and not evil to those who hate us.

One evening while driving my Grand Prix home, the driver behind me was tailgating, flashing his lights at me, and swerving back and forth. I was relieved when I saw he was going to pass, but as he got along side of me, he turned his car toward mine and forced me off the road. My car spun on the soft shoulder before coming to a stop. After I regained my composure, I was furious! I sped onto the road and went after the driver. I caught up to him and forced him off the road as he had done to me. It felt good. No, it felt great. I thought to myself as I drove away, *Now we're even. You forced me off the road, and I did the same to you.* But the other driver didn't see it that way. In my rear view mirror I could see he was in hot pursuit. He caught up with me and pulled in front of me so fast I didn't have time to stop. I plowed into the back end of his car. I jumped out, intending to pull him out of his car and finish what he had started, but he saw me coming and sped away. My "little" retaliation ended up costing $1,972. I learned the hard way to resist the temptation to do unto others as they do unto me. Fortunately, no one was injured.

1 Peter 3:9 says, "Do not repay evil with evil or insult with insult, but with blessing, because to this you were called so that you may inherit a blessing." Teaching our kids to bless those who curse them, to be kind to those who do them evil, is one of the basic elements of Christianity. God doesn't *suggest* we do so; He commands it. Here are three ways to teach the message of 1 Peter 3:9:

1. Take time to walk through cause and effect stories with your kids.
2. Talk about pride and how it affects our relationship with others and with God.
3. Teach a balanced view of what happens when we turn the other cheek.

APPRECIATE PEOPLE

Most of us appreciate the people around us. Our family, friends, church family, and co-workers are all important to us. We enjoy being with them and we're thankful for the things they do for us. It's not that we don't appreciate them; it's that we fail to tell them. Encouragers are people who build those around them, not with a false sense of accomplishment, but with genuine appreciation. They don't look for the negative in people; they focus on the positive.

Our children, and especially our teenagers, need to know we appreciate them for their Christian stand. Many of them encounter tremendous peer pressure to abandon their faith, to rebel against authority, to go with the crowd. As we teach and encourage them in the ways of the Lord, we counteract the assault against them. As we show appreciation for the growth in their lives, we reinforce their determination to serve the Lord.

Appreciation and gratitude go hand in hand. I began to see evidence of both in my son Jeff's life when he came to me with an envelope wanting a stamp. "Who is the letter for? Some girl you met on vacation?" I asked. "No, Dad," he replied, "it's a letter of encouragement for our pastor." I asked if his Sunday school teacher had asked him to write the note. He said, "No, I felt like I was supposed to encourage him and thank him for all he does."

When parents get notes or cards of appreciation from their kids, there's a tendency to wonder if they want something. But children and teenagers are usually far better than adults at expressing their thanks. We tend to get caught up with the busyness of life and assume people know how we feel. So why bother expressing it? Think about how you feel when you receive notes of appreciation. That's the best reason for doing it.

One afternoon I was watching a group of students working and decided to let them know how much I appreciated what they were doing. When I left them, they were working even harder. A little recognition prompted them to exert additional effort.

Appreciation has a way of doing that. It's something we all need; something we all should express. Try expressing appreciation and gratitude to someone in your family every day for the next thirty days. See if it doesn't make a difference in their life and yours. It will change your outlook as you begin to look for the good in those around you.

GIVE A GIFT

The currency of the 1990s is time. It stands to reason that the most valuable thing we can give our family is our time. Most of us, including our kids, don't need more *things*. They need a father to play with, a mother to talk to; they need us. We need to put down the morning newspaper, turn off the television, eliminate distractions, and give of ourselves. Our kids, whatever their age, need to know they're important enough to us to put everything else aside and devote time and attention to them.

Today, more than ever, parents need to learn how to listen to their kids. You may have to get away from the house and create an opportunity and atmosphere for sharing with one another. Take them to lunch, or do something unexpected that costs nothing but your time.

One Sunday afternoon we decided to have a family picnic. That's not uncommon for families, but ours was unique. We held it at the bottom of our pool. We had drained it to acid wash the sides, and for some reason it struck me as a great place for a picnic. Jenna got a blanket, Renee got paper plates, and Jeff filled the cups with ice. My wife thought I was crazy, but it turned out to be great fun. All it took was a little creativity and time.

ENCOURAGE, ENCOURAGE, ENCOURAGE

Every Wednesday night at our youth meeting, a mailbox sits on the back table. A sign on it reads "Mr. Mailbox." The purpose of Mr. Mailbox is for students to write notes of encouragement to one another. They scribble uplifting messages and drop them in the box for delivery. It's proven to be a huge success, as we average nearly one hundred letters each week. The ones who receive the notes are moved and encouraged, and the ones who write them experience the joy. It's been exciting to see them nurtured in the art of encouragement.

I'll never forget the words of encouragement my parents offered when I was growing up. They always knew what to say and when to say it. That hasn't changed. They continue to encourage me and my family today. They were models of encouragement and gave me the gift of their time. Now I'm doing the same with my family. Ask yourself: *Do I want my children to model my style of parenting?* If not, it's never too late to change.

I graduated from high school with a full athletic scholarship. My tenure at the university only lasted a short time, however. When I returned home, I was rehired by the plumbing company I'd worked for in high school. Fred Mauldin, the owner, greatly influenced my life. His work ethic inspired me to be the best I could be and to go the extra mile. His motto was: "You never leave something the way you found it. You leave it better, and then some." Fred's wife is like a second mother to me; their home is always open. They show God's love to everyone around them, and they encourage.

This world needs people like Mrs. Piner, my parents, Fred and Pat Mauldin. Those who have given up on themselves, and there are many, need someone who will continue to believe in them when, like with my bean sprout, nothing promising is evident. They have potential, albeit hidden or buried. But with a little encouragement from someone like Mrs. Piner that person with hidden potential can grow into a person with realized potential.

"May our Lord Jesus Christ himself and God our Father, who loved us and by his grace gave us eternal encouragement and good hope, encourage your hearts and strengthen you in every good deed and word" (2 Thessalonians 2:16,17).

The Reverend Billy Williams is a youth pastor in Visalia, California. He has spent thirteen years working with teens. He and his wife Tonya have three children: Renee, Jeff, and Jenna.

22

Developing Discipline in Kids

STEVE THOMAS

Before we can develop discipline in our kids, we must understand the concept of discipline. The word brings to mind such things as spanking, grounding, or shouting orders. The biblical definition of discipline doesn't mean any of the above; it means "training." Webster also defines discipline as "training intended to elicit a specific pattern of behavior or character; and behavior that results from such training." That's the kind of discipline God talks about in the Bible. He desires us to achieve an excellent lifestyle and character, and He uses discipline to accomplish that in us. God says, "Those whom I love I rebuke and discipline. So be earnest, and repent" (Revelation 3:19).

Though closely linked to love, discipline still conjures up negative feelings. The reason is a lack of understanding. I remember my dad bending me over his knee when I was a child. With his belt poised in mid-air and my backside tightened awaiting the sting, he said, "This is going to hurt me more than it hurts you." I confess, I didn't believe him, but the first time I took my little girl into her room to spank her, I found myself saying and meaning those same words.

It's not fun to discipline our kids. I don't think it's fun for God either when He has to discipline us. We discipline our kids because we know it's best for them, but it's hard knowing they don't understand. As a father of three, I've come to realize they won't understand until they have kids of their own. How do we bear disciplining our children in the meantime? We do it God's way. He loves us enough to correct us even though it hurts because He knows it's necessary. Our gifts will never be used to the fullest until we learn to correct and improve ourselves. We need to teach our children discipline for the same reason.

HELPING OUR KIDS UNDERSTAND DISCIPLINE

If *we* associate discipline with punishment, imagine how much more our kids do. The very word brings negative connotations. Spanking, grounding, privileges revoked, no Nintendo, whatever punishment we use is what our kids will associate with discipline. They see only the immediate displeasure and not the end result. Here are three ways to help them understand discipline.

Communication is the first step to help them understand the need for discipline. Explain what discipline is and how important it is in our lives. I explained to my five-year-old daughter why she had been spanked. I sat down on the edge of her bed and pulled her onto my lap. "Do you know why Mommy and Daddy have to spank?" I asked. Of course she said no. So I explained, "We want you to be good. We want people to like you." Then I asked her to tell me what she had done wrong. That way, the next time she would be able to tell me what she had done and why Mommy and Daddy needed to spank. And, sure enough, when that time came, she answered, "Because of discipline. You want me to learn to be good." Children of all ages need to understand why they're disciplined. They need to know that in order to achieve any desired result, they have to have discipline.

Visualizing desired results is another way to help kids understand discipline. We should help them "read the future." As a youth pastor, I encourage my youth group to look a year down the road. "Project where you want to be," I tell them. "See what you want the desired result to be, and then work to get there." We do that as adults. We set two year goals, five year goals, and so on. While it's more difficult to achieve the goals than to set them, we know we must be disciplined to get anywhere. We may not always practice discipline, but we understand the concept. We need to explain this to our children by applying it to their own situations. For example, if a teenager wants to lose weight, it will take discipline. She can't say, "I want to be thin," and expect it to happen. Losing weight is difficult; she will have to practice discipline to achieve her goal. The same is true with saving money. A teenager will never be able to save money for a down payment on that first car if he spends every dollar he earns. He must be disciplined enough to do without the new sneakers everyone else is wearing. Or perhaps the goal is to read the entire Bible in a year. As teenagers, my brother and I had that goal. We used study guides designed to help us read through the Bible in a year, but we didn't follow them faithfully and, consequently, didn't reach our goal. We need to help our kids visualize future accomplishments so they'll appreciate the discipline needed to achieve the desired results.

DON'T WAIT

It's easier to teach our children discipline when we *start early* in life. Sometimes we don't realize how important this is. There are some disciplines that will not be understood until our children are in their teens. But often they won't be developed if we wait too late to start.

Studies show that by the fourth grade, kids are starting to make decisions about how they feel about their parents, how much they'll listen to what they say, and how much time they want to spend with them. By nature, young children love to be with their parents. But as the teenage years approach, the opposite can occur. It's important we start early on a trusting, loving relationship if we expect our influence to continue into adolescence. It's also about the fourth grade that kids begin to ask Jesus into their lives and to really understand what that means. We shouldn't miss this crucial time to develop spiritual disciplines in them as well.

By the time our kids reach fifteen or sixteen, their attitudes have changed dramatically. Teenagers view their parents as friends more than disciplinarians. If we've developed discipline early, it will be easier to cultivate friendship without sacrificing discipline. The sixteen-year-old who wants Mom to be a friend still needs Mom to guide her.

Another way to help kids understand discipline is by *being an example,* which we'll address later in this chapter.

NITTY-GRITTY DISCIPLINES

Now that we understand discipline and know how to help our kids understand it, we must decide what disciplines we want to develop in them. We must decide what values are important to us, then begin developing them in our children. But there are basic disciplines that every Christian parent should strive to develop in their children. These "nitty-gritty" disciplines fall into two categories: *practical* and *spiritual*.

Spiritual Disciplines. Of the many disciplines we can develop in our children, the following four are very important:

Obedience. The most important discipline we can develop in our children is obedience. If kids don't learn to obey their parents, how will they learn to obey God as teenagers or adults? I was in Bible college trying to write a message entitled "Rules to Christianity" when I first realized the importance of obedience. As I sat at my desk, tapping my pencil against my head, I thought about prayer, worship, and reading God's Word. There must be other rules, I thought. Then it hit me. There's really only one rule, and that's obedience. People say if you pray, everything will fall into place. But if you obey, then you'll pray. Obedience covers it all. We need to discipline our children to become obedient to us and to God. We'll all submit to one authority or another our entire lives. The sooner we understand that, the better.

Devotion. The second spiritual discipline is devotion, which includes three basic elements: prayer, reading God's Word, and worship. A healthy prayer life is important, and therefore we need to teach our kids how to pray. I've had seventeen-year-olds, raised in church, who couldn't pray with me. They haven't been taught how. It's our responsibility as Christian parents to teach them. This includes not just talking to God, but listening to Him as well. We need to help our children develop two-way communication with the Lord at an early age. It's important to know the voice of God. When your child says, "I feel like the Lord spoke to me about . . ." discuss whether or not God would say that. Help them identify God's voice in a clear way.

In addition to prayer, reading the Bible is an important part of our devotional life. God gave us His Word so we can learn about Him and understand the relationship we have with Him. We should make Bible reading a pleasant family experience, but also encourage our children to read the Bible on their own. We should develop enthusiasm in them for God's Word by asking what they've read and allowing them to share with us.

Worship is another vital ingredient of a healthy devotional life. It's disappointing to see kids raised in church not participate in worship in our youth services. They often appear stoical, expressing no emotion, not acknowledging God. I can't understand it until I see some of the parents demonstrating the same lack of devotion. We must teach our children how to worship. We should be broken and humble before the Lord, offering the praise and worship of which He's worthy. Our children need to see that from an early age; they need to know how important Jesus is in our lives. Then they can understand and practice the discipline of worship themselves.

Commitment. The third discipline is that of commitment. We need to raise a generation that is faithfully committed to God. Paraphrasing Matthew 6:33, "Seek first the kingdom of God and His righteousness and all the other things we worry about will be added to us." Committed faithfulness is a fruit of the Spirit. Dr. Robert Laurant, in his book, *Keeping Your Teen in Touch with God,* found that the number one reason teenagers turn away from God and the church after high school is due to a lack of involvement in the church.[1] This is the reason given by young adults who no longer attend church. They're not just talking about a lack of attendance, but a lack of committed involvement. Teens are involved in many activities, but few will have the lasting effect on their adulthood like involvement in church ministry. Committed involvement to the church and the youth group should be a top priority with teens. This discipline should be modeled by committed and involved parents.

Heart and Mind. The fourth discipline we need to develop in our kids is discipline of the heart and mind. The heart and mind are very closely related in the Bible. When we ask God into our heart, He doesn't inhabit the organ that pumps blood, but rather our mind, personality, and spirit. In Philippians 4:8, the apostle Paul gave a list of things on which we need to focus our minds, then said, "think about such things." In Matthew 12:34 Jesus said, "Out of the abundance of the heart the mouth speaks" (NKJV). Knowing that will give us insight into what our kids are thinking about, what they're watching and listening to, and who they're hanging around with. Our minds are like a computer: what goes in, comes out. Because of this, we need to develop in our kids the discipline of guarding their hearts and minds. In other words, they must guard what goes in and balance it with the things of God.

Practical Disciplines. Practical disciplines are spiritual disciplines on a practical level. Again, there are hundreds of disciplines we could choose to develop. The following four are among the most important:

Time Management. The discipline of time goes back to involvement and commitment. Kids have a lot of competing demands between homework, television, church involvement, social activities, and sports events. Time management is essential. We can teach them to organize their time by making and prioritizing lists. I learned to discipline my time the hard way. At age fourteen, it was my job to mow the church lawn. Invariably, I put it off until Saturday. One Saturday, as I was leaving for my job, a group of kids from the youth group called to invite me to go swimming. I couldn't because I had to get my work done. While my friends were swimming, I was mowing. My mother said, "Today you've learned a valuable lesson: business comes before pleasure." That's a lesson all kids need to learn. If they learn to discipline their time, they'll have time for all the important things of life.

Money Management. Another important discipline is money management. Very few adults in our churches tithe. But tithing is an important part of worship, a discipline set forth by God that should be developed in our children. We need to teach them to be good stewards by giving back to God one-tenth of what He's given them and by budgeting their money wisely. To do that, they need to understand the concept of money.

A man once asked, "God, how long is a million years to You?"

"One minute," He replied.

"How much is a million dollars to You?"

"One penny."

"Well, God, may I have a penny?"

"Sure," God replied, ". . . in a minute."

That's often a teenager's perspective of money. They think ten dollars goes a long way when it belongs to their parents, but once it's in their hands, they find it really only buys a couple of burgers at McDonald's. Whenever I take my youth group to the Six Flags amusement park, they spend most of their money on trivial things. Then, invariably, when we stop to eat on the way home, half the kids don't have any money left. They haven't learned the discipline of money management. They haven't learned how to budget. We need to train our kids to be good stewards of their money.

Interpersonal Relationships. The third practical discipline concerns relationships. I meet many teenagers who aren't disciplined in their dating relationships. They don't know how to deal with affection, and that can lead to undisciplined behavior. It's important we teach them how to show affection without compromising God's standards. Discuss godly ways in which affection can be displayed that don't include physical actions.

We need to teach our children respect for others, something many adults also need to learn. If we can teach the value of living by the Golden Rule, which is to "do to others what you would have them do to you" (Matthew 7:12), our children will have no problem in this area of their lives.

We also need to teach the value of choosing good friends. Proverbs 27:17 says, "As iron sharpens iron, so one man sharpens another." Our kids need to have the right kind of friends if they're to have a positive edge.

Learning. The discipline of learning is equally important. I have a sign in my office that reads, "Why didn't life's problems hit me when I was a teenager and still knew everything?" Teenagers may think they know it all, but we know better. They'll discover, as we did, that learning is a lifelong process. For this reason, we need to develop in our kids the value of learning. Learning skills are not always reflected in a child's school grades. For example, a child may earn high grades because of an ability to *memorize,* without actually learning what was taught. Conversely, a child who doesn't perform well on tests may *learn* more than grades reflect. If our kids clearly understand the importance of learning, as opposed to just getting by, and that learning continues throughout life, they'll be better equipped to face the challenges that lie ahead.

FIVE WAYS TO INSTILL DISCIPLINE

Teaching these disciplines to our kids is accomplished, in part, through example, instruction, correction, experience, and accountability.

Example. We instill discipline in our kids by example. This method can be the most difficult *and* the most influential. We've all heard it said, "I can't hear what you say; your actions speak too loudly." It's true, actions speak louder than words. Our walk has to match our talk, especially regarding our Christianity. If we say we're a Christian, we need to act like one. The same applies in modeling discipline. If we say prayer is important, we need to pray. If we say holy living is important, we need to live holy lives. We must set the example if we expect our kids to embrace the values we wish to instill.

I've seen a commercial where a father and son are out for the day. The young boy does everything his father does. When they sit down under a tree the boy crosses his legs just like his dad. Then the dad lights a cigarette and tosses the package down. The boy picks it up, looks at it, and the commercial ends. It's a great message that tells us our kids are watching us. In effect, our actions say, "This is how I want you to live." Kids, and especially teenagers, don't buy the old saying, "Do as I say, not as I do." Many teens are turned off to church and ultimately God because their parents don't act the same at home as they do at church. We must be consistent in the examples we set. The apostle Paul instructed the Corinthians to "follow my example, as I follow the example of Christ" (1 Corinthians 11:1). We should be able to say those same words to our kids.

Instruction. We also instill discipline by instruction. It's not always enough to model certain behavior; it needs to be explained as well. Jesus modeled prayer before His disciples daily, and yet they asked Him to teach them how to pray. (See Luke 11:1.) He *instructed* them through what we call the Lord's Prayer, which was really just an outline He used to explain how they should pray. From it, they acquired principles that helped them develop their own prayer lives.

Regarding God's laws, Deuteronomy 6:7 says, "Impress them on your children. Talk about them when you sit at home and when you walk along the road, when you lie down and when you get up." In other words, take every opportunity to *instruct* them in the ways of God. Explain the whys, the hows, and the rewards. But remember, we must continue to learn ourselves if our instruction is to have lasting value.

Experience is another method by which we instill discipline. It is sometimes difficult to convince our children that something is a mistake when they can't see ahead. We've gained our knowledge through *experience,* but they haven't had the benefit of it yet. When example and instruction fail to get the message across, we have to let them learn by allowing them to make mistakes. Sometimes the lessons can be harsh. A good illustration of this is found in 1 Samuel 15:1-26. Samuel had come to train Saul to be Israel's first king. He gave Saul a word from God telling him to go and completely destroy the Amalekites. He was very precise in saying that Saul was to destroy *everything*. After the battle, God told Samuel that Saul had not done what he was instructed:

> When Samuel reached him, Saul said, "The Lord bless you! I have carried out the Lord's instructions."
>
> But Samuel said, "What then is this bleating of sheep in my ears? What is this lowing of cattle that I hear?"
>
> Saul answered, "The soldiers brought them from the Amalekites; they spared the best of the sheep and cattle to sacrifice to the Lord your God, but we totally destroyed the rest."
>
> "Stop!" Samuel said to Saul. "Let me tell you what the Lord said to me last night."
>
> "Tell me," Saul replied.
>
> Samuel said, "Although you were once small in your own eyes, did you not become the head of the tribes of Israel? The Lord anointed you king over Israel. And he sent you on a mission, saying, 'Go and completely destroy those wicked people, the Amalekites; make war on them until you have wiped them out.' Why did you not obey the Lord? Why did you pounce on the plunder and do evil in the eyes of the Lord?"
>
> "But I did obey the Lord," Saul said. "I went on the mission the Lord assigned me. I completely destroyed the Amalekites and brought back Agag their king. The soldiers took sheep and cattle from the plunder, the best of what was devoted to God,

in order to sacrifice them to the Lord your God at Gilgal."

But Samuel replied: "Does the Lord delight in burnt offerings and sacrifices as much as in obeying the voice of the Lord? To obey is better than sacrifice, and to heed is better than the fat of rams"— 1 Samuel 15:13-22.

God took the kingdom away from Saul because of his disobedience. It wasn't enough that he had been instructed in what God wanted him to do. He learned through experience that obedience was better than sacrifice. But it was too late: he didn't get a second chance. Children who shun example and instruction as a means of developing discipline should be warned that experience is a much harsher teacher.

Correction. Correction is also necessary for discipline to be developed. But correcting is not condemning. It means "to set right, to remedy or to counteract." When our kids make mistakes we need to show them a better way without humiliating them. When our children learn to walk in the physical sense, we don't badger them for tripping over something on the floor. We set them back on their feet, remove the obstacle if we can, and show them how to walk around it if we can't. The same is true in the spiritual sense. As they learn to walk through life we need to correct them, in love, when they trip and fall.

When correction is properly administered, it restores rather than alienates. A child who receives loving correction from a loving parent will not become bitter, and he will not reject the discipline the parent wishes to teach.

Accountability. Finally, accountability helps develop discipline in our children's lives. They must understand that, as children, they're accountable to us. When we give them responsibilities we must hold them accountable to perform their duties. But we must make sure they know what we expect of them. A list of chores is helpful and helps them measure their accomplishments. In training them to be accountable in this area of their lives, we're helping them to become responsible adults.

But accountability doesn't end when they reach adulthood. They will always be accountable to leadership, to authority, and to God, so disciplining them through accountability now is essential. To ensure our children are accountable for their actions, we need to be *aware* of their actions. We have to take an active interest in who they spend time with, what their activities are, and areas in which they experience difficulty. As cited in the account of 1 Samuel 15:1-26, Samuel held Saul accountable for his actions. He made him acknowledge that he had not obeyed God's explicit instructions. When our children, regardless of age, violate the laws we've set for them, we must hold them accountable. It doesn't help them if we overlook their violations or make excuses for them. It only prolongs the lessons they need to learn to live a life that is wholly pleasing to God.

Accountability is two-sided, bringing reward and punishment. As parents, we need to diligently reward the positive and punish the negative. If we allow one or the other to get out of balance, we defeat what we wish to establish.

PROVIDE THE TOOLS

Nothing is more frustrating than trying to do a job without the proper tools. If we're to succeed in teaching disciplines to our children, we need to make sure they're well-equipped. If we want our children to enjoy reading the

Bible, we should get them a version they can understand. Several student Bibles on the market today are excellent tools for teens. If we want to teach our children the discipline of worship, we should get worship tapes they'll enjoy and practice worship in their presence, either through family devotions or in church. If our children need to learn time management, we should require them to begin tasks on time; give them a time frame for completing tasks; and reward them when they achieve specific goals. If they need to learn to budget money, we should set up a budget for them to follow, using their allowance or money earned through a part-time job. We should go over the budget each pay day and make them stay within it. If we want to teach them the discipline of order or organization, we could help them neatly organize their room, then require them to keep it up daily or weekly. We have boxes for our five-year-old daughter's toys and have taught her to put big toys in one box and little toys in another. I've supplied her with shelves for stuffed animals and books. In short, I've equipped her with the tools she needs to keep her room organized.

We also equip our children by giving them responsibility. A good method is the five-step approach:

1. I do it.
2. I do it, you watch.
3. I do it, you do it.
4. I watch while you do it.
5. You do it.

We need to take our children through the whole process with each responsibility we give them. They'll catch on to some more quickly than others, but by completing the process for every situation we ensure they'll be well-equipped to be responsible adults.

DISCIPLINE BRINGS REWARD

In Romans 12:1, the apostle Paul writes, "Therefore, I urge you, brothers, in view of God's mercy, to offer your bodies as living sacrifices, holy and pleasing to God . . ." It requires discipline to accomplish this. Jesus said, "Seek first his kingdom and his righteousness, and all these things will be given to you as well" (Matthew 6:33). This also requires discipline. Any command of God takes discipline. Yet discipline, when developed, brings reward. Discipline is the pathway to achievement. It's the "no pain, no gain" philosophy.

Disciplining our children can be agonizing and exhausting. Hebrews 12:6 says, ". . . the Lord disciplines those he loves, and he punishes everyone he accepts as a son." If we truly love our children we must do the same. Disciple is the root word of discipline. When Jesus invited someone to be His disciple, He was actually saying, "Come and be My disciplined follower." The most important responsibility we'll ever have as parents is to help our children become disciplined followers of Jesus Christ. The rewards of such discipline are eternal.

The Reverend Steve Thomas is a youth pastor at Canyon Hills Assembly in Bakersfield, California. His youth group has grown from thirty to more than two hundred during his tenure. Steve is a conference speaker and has written a leadership training manual entitled Explosive Youth Strategies.

He and his wife Debbie have three children: Tristen, Blake, and Jordan.

23
Whatever Happened to Values?

BARRY SAPPINGTON

For four consecutive years I was invited to speak to the sophomore health class of a local high school on the topic of values. Knowing how sensitive the public school system is, I would carefully prepare my presentation each year so as not to be offensive to anyone.

I opened my speech with an illustration that in America if a person is convicted of stealing a bald eagle's egg out of its nest and killing the embryo, he would be fined $5,000 and sentenced to six months in jail. But, in most cities across America, a young lady can get an abortion without parental consent and without fear of being punished. I pointed out that the life of an eagle has taken precedence over the life of a child growing in its mother's womb.

At the conclusion of my values presentation, an outraged high school health teacher approached me with anger in her words. I could hardly believe what was spewing from her lips. She wondered how I dared suggest that abortion is wrong. I wanted to shout, "Because it is! God's Word says so!" But I restrained myself and listened as she vehemently presented *her* viewpoint. Needless to say, she was convinced women have a right to choose the fate of their unborn child, and she didn't want her students exposed to an opposing opinion.

Where are the values our country was founded on? Are they still ingrained within our children, or are they lost forever? Unless we see a spiritual awakening in America, it will be difficult to restore the moral fabric that wove this country together. For believers in the Lord Jesus Christ, there are specific ways to teach our children how to develop values in accordance with God's Word.

RELATIVISM VS. ABSOLUTES

In many American homes, including those of Christians, values are not represented for the young person to model. I have asked individuals who lived through World War II and the Korean War, "Were you taught moral absolutes as a child?" The response is always a resounding yes. They said the same problems that exist today were, to some degree, present during their upbringing. They cheated on tests, went to parties where alcohol was available, and were sexually active. But they were quick to add that the problems were not as widespread.

Teens today are tempted with the same things faced by young people of thirty years ago. The only difference is that more are acting on the temptations and getting away with it. We've lifted the restraints and, in turn, values have gone by the wayside. Many teens have no concept of purity and morality.

For the past three decades we've experienced an erosion of morality and a lack of support for the value system that made this country great. Families are dying, primarily because we have rejected the values of our forefathers in favor of a philosophy of relativism. There are no more absolutes.

For many years our country has been shifting from a society of values to a society calloused to sin. What used to be considered sinful is now tolerated. Perhaps the only nationally recognized sin remaining is that of *intolerance*. This should cut deep into the heart of the believer, for this philosophy suggests the real sinner is one who believes in a godly standard of behavior. On the other hand, those who cheat on their spouse, have premarital sex, or have an abortion are considered normal. Believers are labeled extremist and ultraconservative for championing the cause of morality.

I read where a baseball game being played by inner-city youth was interrupted in the fourth inning by a murder. A neighborhood drug dealer was gunned down by a rival who wanted his marketing turf. As the boys watched the murder take place, they became anxious and frustrated, not because a young man was gunned down, but because the police interrupted their game. How indicative this is of a society devaluing human life. Because of moral and ethical decisions made by their parents, today's youth have been loaded on a high speed train traveling across the land, out of control, destroying every obstacle or value it comes across. It's time for the train to get a new Conductor with a new destination. That's what God longs to do, but He is waiting for parents and the Church to make a stand for biblical values.

Our children are bombarded with messages from the media. Through television, radio, records, tapes, CDs, and magazines our youth are indoctrinated with the message of relativism. Few families escape the influence and repercussion of media-philosophies. Influenced by what we watch on television, we say and do things we've learned from a value-less system. Our ability to communicate truth and combat impure thoughts is diminished. The old adage "garbage in, garbage out" is apropos for the influence the media is having on young people and families.

VALUE CLARIFICATION

There is a move in our public secondary schools today toward "value clarification." Because of the condition of students and public schools as a whole, scholars are now advancing the concept of teaching students the importance of character, integrity, and virtue. Indeed, these values are biblical in nature, and when taken at face value, it sounds good to teach our kids right and wrong. But without *something* acting as a standard, what constitutes "wrong" becomes merely a matter of opinion.

Hope for society is found in the eternal Word of God. God gave us the Ten Commandments to be the standard for our actions. Christ took it a step further.

> Jesus replied, "'Love the Lord your God with all your heart and with all your soul and with all your mind.' This is the first and greatest commandment. And the second is like it: 'Love your neighbor as yourself.' All the Law and the Prophets hang on these two commandments"—Matthew 22:37-40.

Our courts, however, have banned the ten commandments from public schools along with the rest of God's Word. What then is the standard for this present generation?

TRUE VALUE CLARIFICATION

Webster's Dictionary defines *value* as "something (like that of a certain principle or quality), intrinsically valuable or desirable."[1] In other words, values are principles that are esteemed as being highly desirous. Parents are primarily responsible for the transference of values and standards that their children can emulate. Those standards must be established and adhered to based on the Word of God. Dr. Haim Ginott says, "A parent's responsibility is not to his child's happiness; it's to his character."[2] What a challenge to parents, to raise and train our children in the ways of Christ. Too often we attempt to make our children happy by providing the material items they *think* they need, and cheat them out of what they *truly* need, which is good character. The values instilled in them are manifested by a reputation that reflects moral excellence.

These values are developed over a period of years, beginning at birth and continuing throughout adolescence. Primarily they are instilled during the early formative years, then challenged at adolescence. If parents do their part to teach biblical values at an early age, the chances are good their child will maintain a life based on values and manifested through character. Proverbs 4:11 says, "I would have you learn this great fact: that a life of doing right is the wisest life there is" (TLB).

How does a parent instill values and character into children? Before that question can be addressed, parents should consider these questions:

What kind of person am I? Many would say they grew up in homes where they were not taught values that reflected the standard of Christ. Instead, they were taught cultural values. In turn, children will reflect parental values demonstrated to them. Bruno Bettelheim says, "The only way morals can be taught (to children) is through the moral life of the parents."[3] As the father of two children, I recognize the responsibility of knowing my daughter and son will become what my wife and I are. How do I rate in the following areas:

Acceptance of People. Am I prejudiced? Do I criticize people I don't know or who are different from me? Do I show respect for strangers? Would my children say I am accepting of people?

Conflict Management. Do I deal with tension when it arises, or do I hold grudges? Do I share my feelings in a constructive manner during conflict, bent on reconciliation? Do I take action to better a situation once conflict is resolved?

Faith. Do my children see my commitment to God? Are spiritual matters discussed in my home? Do we go to church as a family? Would my children say I have a strong faith?

Integrity. Do I exaggerate stories when talking to friends? Do I lie in order to get out of conversations on the phone? Do I always tell the truth about my children's ages, even if it costs me more money? Would my child say I'm honest?

Love. Do I openly express affection? Do I place conditions placed on my expressions of love? Do my children see that I love my spouse? Would my children say I'm a loving person?

Servanthood. Do I rush to be first in line? Do I help clean up after an event or party? Do I always have to sit in the front seat of the car? Am I comfortable sharing my belongings? Would my children describe me as a servant?

What kind of person is my child? This question will force me to evaluate what my children consider important, what they value. Do they reflect values in line with God and His Word? Children who mature into stable adults commonly have a caring parent who has been a positive role model, one who has taken time to evaluate themselves and their children on an ongoing basis, making sure everyone stays on track. Here are some questions to help us gauge where our children are in the development of godly character:

What are my children's interests? This is a significant question when attempting to evaluate their values. Are they interested in godly activities? Do they place too much emphasis on members of the opposite sex? What kind of music do they listen to? What kind of friends do they have?

How much do my children reflect their culture? Do they demand brand name clothing? Do they watch a great deal of television? What types of movies do they like? What kind of language do they use?

What kind of faith do they display? Do they want to please the Lord? Do they like to attend church? Do they have a passion to uphold the standard of Christ?

Do they have integrity? Are they honest? Do they exaggerate the truth in order to win favor with their friends? Do they hide things from me?

How do they express love? Can they express affection freely? Do they love others genuinely? Are they emotional or unemotional?

What kind of person is God? The answer to this question is vital, for God is the source of the values we desire to instill in our children. We should try to emulate four particular attributes of God as examples for our children:

Holy. The holiness of God is a recurring theme in the Old Testament. Isaiah 6:1-3 speaks of God's incredible holiness: "Holy, holy, holy is the Lord Almighty; the whole earth is full of His glory!" Moses, Job, and Isaiah all had visions of the holiness and perfection of God. Leviticus 11:43-45 says, "Be holy, because I am holy."

Righteous. God always does what is righteous and just. He reveals His righteousness and justice by rewarding the righteous (see Hebrews 6:10 and 2 Timothy 4:8) and in many other ways so that after the Judgment no one can say they do not deserve their sentence. (See Revelation 16:5,6.) God forgives the repentant. (See 1 John 1:9.) He keeps His word and promises to His children. (See Nehemiah 9:7,8.)

Merciful and Kind. He is a God of mercy, willing to withhold punishment. His kindness leads Him to bless His obedient children. A wonderful reward and blessing await those who uphold His standard. God's mercy and kindness is illustrated in the parable of the Prodigal Son. (See Luke 15:11-32.) The prodigal son had been influenced by the culture of his day. He left a secure home to pursue the pleasures of the world. It was fun for a season, but when the money was spent, he ended up in a pigpen. With no money and no place to go, he returned home. His father welcomed him with open arms and gave him a feast. The father had the right to deal harshly with his son. Instead, he bestowed mercy on his son, giving him what he didn't deserve. That sounds like our God. "He is merciful and tender toward those who don't deserve it; he is slow to get angry and full of kindness and love" (Psalm 103:8, TLB).

Loving. Christianity is one of few religions that has a Supreme Being of love. Other religions have gods who are angry and hateful, always needing to be appeased. First John 4:8-16 says that God is love. He loved us so much "that he gave his only Son so that anyone who believes in him shall not perish but have eternal life" (John 3:16, TLB). God has such a constant interest in the physical and spiritual welfare of His people that He is compelled to make sacrifices beyond human understanding to reveal His love. He is the ultimate expression of love.

WHAT'S MISSING?

As parents, we're concerned that our children reflect the right values. We're faced with a great challenge to help our young people focus on what is really important in life—and that's *being,* not *doing.* We can ask the Holy Spirit to reveal God's greatness to our children and to allow His light to guide them to what is truly valuable in life. We must continually evaluate where our children are, then keep them moving toward the character of God, eliminating undesirable character traits along the way.

Our society is lacking in four major areas today, perhaps because parents have neglected to instill these values in their children:

Morality. The moral fiber of America has been shredded by the liberal perspective on issues such as premarital sex, abortion, pornography, homosexuality, and incest. In thirty years, our country has declined into moral chaos.

The television show "20/20" recently aired a segment entitled "The Menstrual Extraction." This is an increasingly popular home abortion device. I wept as I watched the program. They performed an abortion by using the menstrual extraction process. The woman who had designed and performed the process looked into the glass container that held the extracted fluid from the woman's uterus and exclaimed, "I think we got it all." I couldn't believe how insensitive they were about what we know was the death of a seven-week-old fetus. Our schools say, "Use condoms." Our families say, "Get an abortion; we don't have time or money to raise another child." The women of this country say, "It's my body, and I can do whatever I want with it." What happened to America's sense of morality?

Christian youth are having sex and engaging in other immoral acts almost on the same scale as teens outside the church. This is happening because believers have brought the values of the world into the church. In Romans 12:1,2, the apostle Paul urges us not to emulate the behavior and customs of the world. He challenges us to allow God to transform our spirits and find true fulfillment in the ways of the Father. If we who comprise the body of Christ, especially parents, don't begin to look at our own moral conduct, how can we expect our teens to behave differently than their non-Christian peers? We must demonstrate a standard of holiness, patterning our lives after the attributes of God. Then our young people will have a genuine role model that follows Christ.

To instill morality in our children, we must begin by determining their level of morality. This evaluation can be made by first considering their conduct as it relates to Scripture. The Bible is filled with moral absolutes that are contrary to cultural mandates. We should discuss issues such as dating, premarital sex, and abortion with our teens.

They must know we care enough to ask, "How can I help?" and "What can I do to help you understand what is right and wrong concerning moral issues?" This topic of conversation may not be easy to conduct with our teens at first, but it is important that we get beyond our shyness and deal with these issues face to face. It could make all the difference in how our young people conduct themselves, which could make all the difference in the direction their lives take.

Integrity. This value is missing in our culture. Too often we read or hear about those in leadership positions from pastors to presidents who have engaged in illegal or immoral behavior. No wonder our young people lack character and integrity. Integrity is what others see in us. It displays a lifestyle that's been proven over time and is consistent with the Word of God. It seems to be a rare thing today to find an individual who's respected for his or her integrity. We are afraid to place our confidence in someone in leadership because of the lack of integrity we find in society.

Integrity must be developed in the formative years of a child. To help build integrity in a child we must encourage "right thinking" by discussing with them various acts of dishonesty we read about in the newspaper or see on the local news. We can help our children discern the motives of the perpetrators and compare their actions with the biblical perspective. Role playing is another way to teach children integrity. Use real life situations to give a clear definition of right and wrong actions. For example, act out cheating on a test, using a fake ID, or lying to a parent. Discuss the consequences of dishonesty, especially the way it damages a relationship. Share how one lie can lead to another in order to cover up the first lie. If we can teach our children the importance of honesty, which is the root of integrity, we can help them experience healthy relationships in their home, school, marriage, community, and government.

Respect. I was taught the value of showing people respect. I was taught to call my minister "Pastor." If I dared call him by his first name, my backside would have been blistered. Today, however, many young people are very familiar with the adults in their lives. "Pastor," "Sir," and "Ma'am" are not a part of their vocabulary. Manners and respect for people are virtually non-existent in some parts of our country, and young people are being taught (by the media in particular) to challenge authority. That doesn't dismiss our responsibility to teach our children respect as it relates to their peers, families, and authority figures; it merely intensifies it.

Scripture instructs us to respect three areas of authority. First is the absolute authority that belongs to God. Moral law begins with Him, and laws of nature express His authority in the natural realm. Second, we are to respect the authority provided by the U. S. Constitution. This authority is based on the consensus of those who live democratically under its control. Government, public education, the military, public service officials, and representatives have authority because it's been given to them. Third is the area of delegated authority, conferred by a higher power. A police officer, for example, can make an arrest because he has been given authority by a higher law and power.

The Bible has much to say about respect: for mother and father (see Leviticus 19:3); for the elderly (see Leviticus 19:32); for husband and wife (see Ephesians 5:33); for our earthly masters (see Ephesians 6:5); for deacons (see

1 Timothy 3:8); for those who need an answer with regard to Jesus (see 1 Peter 3:15).

Responsibility. To be responsible is to be reliable, trustworthy, and stable. It sounds much like integrity, but unfortunately it's difficult to find teens who are responsible. Commitment to God goes much further than a verbal response of "come into my heart." It involves responsibility. When we commit to the kingdom of God, we commit to being responsible and faithful to the commands of God. Is this the case in our homes, our churches, our schools? We beg for people to be committed to ministries in the church. We plead for workers to help with projects only to have three or four show up to help paint or clean the church. They're reliable, however, when we announce an activity that appeals to them. Teens have been programmed to believe that if a cause doesn't involve compensation or personal gain, there's no reason to be responsible to it. It's been suggested that twenty percent of a church congregation does eighty percent of the work. Teens have assimilated that lack of commitment to the body of Christ and allowed it to affect other areas in their lives.

In Luke 19:17, Jesus tells the parable of the master and his servant: "Well done, my good servant! . . . Because you have been trustworthy in a very small matter, take charge of ten cities." Those who have been faithful and responsible in the Lord's service will be richly rewarded in heaven. What a great hope we have. We need to teach our children how to be responsible by demonstrating responsibility. We'll all reap the benefits.

The youth of America are facing a values crisis, treading water in a tumultuous sea of doubt and confusion. Parents must be in the water with them, ready to guide them to the Life Preserver of their Savior, Jesus Christ, if they're to survive. Once they fall in love with Jesus, they'll embrace His values.

Our primary responsibility to our children is to live a Christ-honoring life, to have His values evident in our words and actions. That is how we will develop values in our children. Remember, "a parent's responsibility is not to his child's happiness; it's to his character."

The Reverend Barry Sappington, an ordained Assemblies of God minister, is student ministries pastor at Bethel Church in San Jose, California. He graduated from Trinity Life Bible College and has been involved in youth ministry in Northern California for eleven years. He is a highly touted youth speaker at camps and conventions.

He and his wife Kandee have two children.

24

The Family Game Plan

LARRY RUST

I discovered a spiritual truth, of all places, in the comic strip "Peanuts." A disappointed Charlie Brown finds himself sitting on top of the baseball mound after a game muttering these words, "One hundred and forty to nothing. . . . I just don't understand it . . . and we were so sincere." We want what is best for our children, but sincerity alone doesn't guarantee success. A loving home increases the chances that our children will have a positive relationship with God, but we must have a plan to develop that relationship. As author Chuck Swindoll writes, "The church seldom resurrects what the home puts to death."[1]

PLAN OF ATTACK

My oldest son Eric and I enjoy the sport of rock climbing. We understand successful climbing depends on a good plan. In fact, the climber's motto is "You must stay on route." One weekend Eric and I decided to forge our own route up a particular cliff. Eric said, "Okay, Dad, let's go up the dihedral, traverse right fifteen feet, down-climb ten feet over this ledge and set up Station One. Then we'll go up the second pitch to the 5.7-5.8 hard crack to the top." That's exactly what we did, for climbers never divert from their plans unless they plan the diversion. They stay with their game plan, establishing anchors, protection, care, confidence, assurance, trust, and commitment. That ensures success, or as climbers call it, "flash" or "red point."

It's been said, "If you fail to plan, you plan to fail." That certainly holds true for the family. Goals are not accomplished by hoping, by osmosis, by mental assent, or even sincerity. Why then do many parents believe their children will develop life principles in these ways? There must be an evaluated, calculated, self-determined plan for the eternal destiny of our children's lives. We must develop a family plan and not get off route.

Billy Sunday, the great evangelist of a past generation, spoke these last words to his wife: "Ma, the tragedy of my life is that although I've led thousands of people to Jesus Christ, my own sons are not saved." One of his sons became an atheist and died an alcoholic not because his father was insincere or ungodly, but because he didn't devote enough time to his family. My family is so important to me that years ago I developed a "family game plan" so such a thing wouldn't happen.

What do you want for your children? Have you and your spouse discussed this question? A survey asked parents to list five traits they wanted their children to possess. The results were that sixty-three percent wanted their kids to have a sense of responsibility, forty-nine percent said good manners, forty-five percent said tolerance, thirty-six percent said a meaningful faith, and twenty-nine percent said a sense of independence.[2] My wife and I decided to make our own list of the traits we want our two sons to possess:

Godliness. We want them to know and obey God. I've explained to them their obedience to their mother and me is a prelude to obeying God. If they will obey us, it will be much easier for them to obey God.

Honesty. Satan is called the father of lies. (See John 8:44.) If we call ourselves Christians, honesty and truthfulness must be a part of our character.

Responsibility. I want my sons to be responsible in life. That includes taking responsibility for the choices they make, right or wrong, without passing the buck.

A positive attitude. After church one evening, my son Adam said, "Dad, you sure did preach long." I thought about that a moment, then asked him to be more positive in his statement. He responded, "Dad, I'm positive you preached long." That wasn't exactly what I had in mind, but as I thought about the episode, it made me realize for my children to have a positive attitude in life they need to see it in me.

A positive self-image. Few things are more important than a healthy self-image, and few things are more disgusting than an *over*-healthy one. When we truly understand our position in Christ there's little danger that it will be too low or too high. When balanced, our self-image will carry us through the rough places in life.

What is *your* plan of attack? If you haven't made one, write down five traits you want to see developed in your children. Then sit down with your children and talk about them. That's developing a game plan. Mertan Strommen said, "A committed, intrinsic Christian faith is best communicated by adults who are not only accurate in their empathetic relationships, but also gospel oriented in their faith. In other words, openness and perceptiveness with respect to one's children are highly associated with a similar religious faith in young people."[3]

FIVE GIFTS FOR OUR CHILDREN

Time. How do you spell love? T-I-M-E. Our children are young only once, and that's when they need us most! Moses told Jewish parents to seize every opportunity to convey God's laws and precepts to their youngsters: when they sat down together, when they walked together, before they went to bed, and when they got up in the morning. If a tidy house is more important than having fun with our kids, perhaps our priorities are out of balance. If gaining and maintaining a high standard of living leaves no time for nurturing, maybe the cost is too high. Today's fast pace, the pressure to succeed, and the lure of materialism conspire to sap us of the emotional energy needed to build relationships with our children. "If I can't spend a quantity of time, then I'll spend *quality* time" has been a convenient slogan for busy parents. But our kids need more of our time. We should make a conscious decision to make time with them a high priority.

Living our convictions. A study showed if both mother and father attend church regularly seventy-two percent of the children remain faithful to God; fifty-five percent if only the father attends regularly; fifteen percent if only the mother attends regularly; and six percent if neither attend regularly. Notice the tremendous response when the father faithfully attends church. Dr. James Dobson stated, "If America is going to survive, it will be because husbands and fathers begin to put their families at the highest level of priorities and reserve something of their time, effort, and energy for leadership within their own homes."[4] Our lives must be consistent before our children.

Unconditional love. In the Psalms, David lovingly praised God for His long-suffering attitude toward persistent rebellion. In Hosea, God reiterates His unconditional love by using the example of a prophet who married a harlot and faithfully loved her despite her repeated adultery.

I talked with a young man who grew up being loved *if* he did good. He said he knew the words to say and the way to act to his benefit, but in the long run, he rebelled. Our children should receive worth by birth. Unconditional love will provide security and help ward off rebellion. Do we love our children because of performance, behavior, career choices, potential, or need? Or do we love them because they're ours, with no strings attached? They can answer those questions quickly and accurately, even if we can't. God loves us unconditionally; we owe it to our ki to do the same.

Training. Training is more than teaching. Proverbs 22:6 says, "Train a child in the way he should go, and when he is old he will not turn from it." Webster defines *train* as: "To mold the character, instruct by exercise, drill, to make obedient, put or point in an exact direction, or, to prepare for a contest."[5] Also notice the result of training with discipline. Hebrews 12:11 says, "All discipline for the moment seems not to be joyful, but sorrowful; yet to those who have been trained by it, afterwards it yields the peaceful fruit of righteousness" (NASB).

A game plan plays a vital role in the training of our children. One of the best activities in our family has been our father-son getaways. When they reached ages 5-6, 11-12, 15-16, and 18-19, I would take each son on a trip. They provided opportunities for serious conversation and for the pleasure of being together.

When Eric was eleven years old we took a trip to Yosemite Valley. We backpacked up Mist Trail to Little Yosemite Valley, pitched our tent by a stream, and enjoyed the night under the stars. The next day we hiked to the top of Half Dome. As we sat looking out over the valley, we talked about issues relevant to Eric. We discussed girls, sex, future goals, and, ultimately, his personal relationship with Jesus Christ. It was a great day, but it didn't happen by chance.

When Adam was twelve we found our way to Burney Falls State Park. We prepared camp under a full moon and listened to the crickets sing. We sat on a log with a cold drink and had "one of those talks." Once again, the trip didn't happen by chance. I planned it for the purpose of "training my child."

Right now would be a good time to plan a special trip with your kids. It could be a camping trip, a trip to see a ball game, a father/daughter date. Plan it around your interests, but *plan it*. Whatever it costs in money, time, and effort, it's the best investment you can make.

Respect. Someone has said that the toughest thing about raising kids is convincing them who has seniority. We can't abdicate our authority, but we can and should show respect to our kids. We do so by recognizing that children are not carbon copies of one other. We must allow them to be individuals.

We must also respect their opinions even when they differ from ours. It's okay to say no, and sometimes it's imperative that we do so. But we shouldn't deny them the privilege of having and expressing their own opinion.

Finally, we all have pressures in life, but we can't be so shortsighted as to think our kids don't have them as well. We need to respect the difficulties they face and make ourselves available to them. If we aren't there to ease the pressures they go through, they'll find ways of their own, perhaps through alcohol, drugs, or illicit sex.

Our children will grow up with or without a game plan, but how successfully depends on how much we choose to invest in them.

The Reverend Larry Rust is senior pastor of Susanville Assembly of God and creator of Time Net Management, a pastoral time management program. He has been in pastoral ministry for twenty years. A gifted speaker, he is a graduate of Bethany College where he majored in Biblical Studies.

He and his wife Hilda have two sons: Eric and Adam.

About the Editors

Hal Donaldson is a journalism graduate of San Jose State University. He served as editor of *On Magazine* and taught at Bethany College. He is president of ChurchCare Network, an organization that sends ministries—at no cost—to smaller churches. He has authored numerous books, including *Where is the Lost Ark?*, *One Man's Compassion*, *Treasures in Heaven*, and *Downfall: Secularization of a Christian Nation*.

Kenneth M. Dobson left a successful business career to enter full-time ministry many years ago. He received his B. A. in Biblical Literature from Northwest College and his M. A. in Church Leadership from Southern California College. He formerly served with Mark and Huldah Buntain in Calcutta, India. He is the pastor of First Assembly of God in Visalia, California—a thriving congregation of more than 1,500. The Reverend Dobson's first book is entitled, *The Vow*.

For order information write:

Onward Books
P. O. Box 292305
Sacramento, CA 95829.

Endnotes

Chapter 1

1. On May 14, 1988, Larry Mahoney, under the influence of alcohol, drove his pickup down the wrong side of an interstate highway near Carrolton, Kentucky. He crashed head-on into a church bus bringing 67 young people and their sponsors home from a day at an amusement park. The bus belonged to First Assembly of God in Radcliff, Kentucky. Twenty-seven people died; dozens more were crippled and scarred.
2. Children's Defense Fund. Figures are daily averages based on annual figures. Some statistics are from 1988 census data. Other figures are derived from annual crime reports and other information dating from 1985 to 1988.

Chapter 2

1. Norman Wright, *The Power of a Parent's Word* (Ventura: Regal Books, 1991), p. 298.

Chapter 3

1. Patrick M. Morley, *The Man in the Mirror* (Brentwood, TN: Wolgemuth & Hyatt, 1989), p. 89.
2. Charles L. Allen, *The Secret of Abundant Living* (Old Tappan, NJ: Fleming H. Revell, 1980), p. 21.

Chapter 4

1. Dudley Weeks, *The Eight Essential Steps to Conflict Resolution* (Los Angeles, CA: Jeremy P. Tarcher, Inc., 1992), p. 4.
2. Dr. William Henricks, *How to Manage Conflict* (Shawnee Mission, KS: National Press Publications, 1991), p. 3.

3. Ibid.
4. Weeks, *Eight Essential Steps*, p. 91,92,120,121,161,162.
5. Ibid., p. 175,176.
6. Henricks, *How to Manage Conflict*, p. 20.

Chapter 7

1. Margaret Baker, *Wedding Customs and Folklore* (Totowa, NJ: Rowman and Littlefield, 1977), p. 23,36,37.
2. Paul Olson, *Distinctively Christian Marriage* (Chowchilla, CA: Family Strategies, 1992), 131 S. 3rd St. Chowchilla, CA 1-800-842-8618).

Chapter 8

1. A. W. Tozer, *Of God and Men* (Harrisburg, PA: Christian Publication, Inc., 1960), p. 14,16.

Chapter 9

1. James S. Hewett, *Illustrations Unlimited* (Wheaton, IL: Tyndale House Publishers, Inc., 1988), p. 131.

Chapter 11

1. John Nesbet & Patricia Oberdeen, *Megatrends 2000* (Avon Books), Introduction, xxi.
2. Ibid, p. 23.
3. Ibid, p. 136.
4. Ibid, p. 138.
5. *USA Today* "Coke, IBM, put their brands on the world," November 15, 1988.
6. *Megatrends 2000*, p. 119.
7. Ibid, p. 129.
8. R. B. Reich, *The Work of Nations* (New York, 1990), p. 3,4.
9. Robert Hughes, *Culture of Complaint* (Oxford University Press, 1993), p. 7.
10. *Los Angeles Times*, March 23, 1992, p. 83.
11. "Teenage Pregnancies in Industrialized Countries," *Seattle Times*, April 23, 1989.
12. Ann Rosewater, *Children and Family Trends* (New York Academy of Political Science, 1989), p. 4.
13. *New York Times*, July 6, 1990 and March 19, 1991.

14. *Washington Times*, Georgianne Guyers, February 27, 1989.
15. Hughes, *Culture of Complaint*, p. 28.
16. Ibid., p. 79.
17. Alice in Chains, "Dirt," Hal Leonard Publishing Corp., Milwaukee, WI, 1993.
18. Paul Kennedy, *Preparing for the 21st Century* (New York: Random House, 1993).
19. Ibid., p. 37.
20. Ibid., p. 46.
21. Ibid., p. 348,349.

Chapter 12

1. Nancy Gibbs, "Teaching kids about sex," *Time Magazine*, May 24, 1993, p. 61.
2. Ibid.
3. Ibid.
4. Ibid, p. 62.
5. Ibid.
6. *Today's Teens: A Generation in Transition*, (Glendale, CA: The Barna Research Group, Glendale, 1991).
7. Jay Kesler, *Ten Mistakes Parents Make with Teenagers* (Brentwood, TN: Wolgemuth & Hyatt, 1988), p. 49.
8. Scott Kirby, *Dating: Guidelines for the Bible* (Grand Rapids, MI: Baker Book House, Grand Rapids, 1991), p. 2,3.
9. Ibid.
10. Ibid, p. 13,14.
11. Josh McDowell and Paul Lewis, *Givers, Takers and Other Kinds of Lovers* (Wheaton, IL: Tyndale House Publishers, 1979), p. 94,95.
12. Ibid., p. 13,14.
13. Rich Wilkerson, *Teenagers, Parental Guidance Suggested* (Eugene, OR: Harvest House Publishers, 1983), p. 103.
14. Josh McDowell and Dick Day, *Why Wait* (San Bernardino, CA: Here's Life Publishers, 1987), p. 18.
15. Tim Stafford, "Waiting for love in a hurry up world," *Campus Life*, May 1984, p. 34.
16. McDowell and Day, *Why Wait*, p. 279.

Chapter 13

1. Dawson McAllister, *Please Don't Tell My Parents* (Dallas: Word Publishers, 1992), p. 70.
2. Ibid., p. 13,67,52,89.

Chapter 14

1. Charles R. Swindoll, *Growing Wise in Family Life* (Portland, OR: Multnomah Press, 1988), p. 39.
2. Ibid.
3. Kenneth S. Wuest, *Treasures from the Greek New Testament for the English Reader* (Grand Rapids, MI: William B. Eerdmans Publishing Company, 1941), p. 18.
4. Jay Kesler with Ronald A. Beers, *Parents & Teenagers* (Wheaton, IL: SP Publications, Inc., 1984), p. 242.
5. Charles R. Swindoll, *Strike the Original Match* (Portland, OR: Multnomah Press, 1980), p. 46.

Chapter 15

1. Michael G. Maudlin, *Christianity Today*, "Hollywood vs. America," March 8, 1993, p. 23.
2. Michael Medved, *Hollywood vs. America* (New York: Harper Collins Publishing, Inc., 1992), p. 4.
3. Maudlin, *Christianity Today*, p. 23.
4. Medved, *Hollywood vs. America*, p. 111.
5. B. W. Kilbourne, J. W. Buehler, M. F. Rogers, "AIDS as a Cause of Death in Children, Adolescents, and Young Adults," *American Journal of Public Health*, 80:499, April 1990.
6. Maudlin, *Christianity Today*, p. 23.
7. Ibid.
8. James Dobson, *Focus on Family*, September 1992.
9. Leonard Eron and L. Rowell Huesmann, eds., *Television and the Aggressive Child* (New Jersey: L. Erlbaum, 1986), James Dobson, *Focus on the Family*, September 1992.
10. Ted Baehr, *Christianity Today*, August 17, 1992.
11. Michael Medved, *Focus on the Family*, March 1993.
12. Maudlin, *Christianity Today*, p. 25.
13. Tipper Gore, *Raising PG Kids in an X-Rated Society* (Nashville: Abingdon Press, 1987), p. 29.
14. Larry E. Greeson, *Journal of Applied Social Psychology*, 1991, V. H. Winston & Son, Inc. p. 1909.
15. Ibid.
16. Ibid.
17. Ibid.
18. Richard Lacayo, "Cult of Death," *Time Magazine*, March 15, 1993, p. 36-39.

19. Jeffrey Arnett, "Adolescents and Heavy Metal Music," *Youth and Society*, Vol. 23 No. 1, September 1991, p. 84.
20. Ibid., p. 85.
21. Jill Leslie Rosenbaum and Lorraine Prinsky, "The Presumption of Influence: Recent Response to Popular Music Subcultures," *Crime and Delinquincy*, Vol. 37 No. 4, October 1991, p. 529.
22. Gore, *Raising PG Kids*, p. 41.
23. Nelson Price, "Pornography and Sexual Violence: Booming Business Victimizing Children, Women and Men," *Engage/Social Action* (July/August 1985), p. 13.
24. James Dobson, "The Second Great Civil War," *Focus on the Family*, November 1990.

Chapter 17

1. Merrill, Dean, *The Loving Leader: A Man's Role at Home* (Arcadia, CA: Focus on the Family, 1983), p. 15.
2. Fleming, Jean, *A Mother's Heart* (Colorado Springs, CO: NavPress, 1982), p. 159.

Chapter 18

1. Paul E. Paino, *Questions and Answers*.
2. Barbara Beach and Ann Carr, "Teenagers Today," p. 8-12. Reprinted with permission. *GROUP Magazine*, 1987, GROUP Publishing, P. O. Box 481, Loveland, CO 80539.

Chapter 19

1. William Lane, *Word Biblical Commentary* (Dallas, TX: Word Books Publisher, 1991), Vol. 47a, p. 81.

Chapter 20

1. Story told by Tom Green, D-CAP of Wyoming, at Youth Alive Conference in Fort Worth, TX (1992).
2. 1984 Equal Access Act, Title VIII of the Public Law 98-377.
3. Used by permission from Roever Communications.
4. This testimony can be verified by Debra Garten Masto, Club Advisor, 217 Walnut Street, Apt. 3, Clarksburg, WV 26301.

5. "Take a Stand" campus manual. Youth Alive Department, 1445 Boonville Avenue, Springfield, MO 65802.

6. "Students' Legal Rights," by J. W. Brinkley, can be purchased from Dave Roever Communications, P.O. Box 136130, Fort Worth, TX 76136, (817) 238-2005.

Chapter 22

1. Robert Laurant, *Keeping Your Teen in Touch With God* (Elgin, IL: David C. Cook, 1988).

Chapter 23

1. *Webster's Dictionary*, (G & C Merriam Company, 1973).

2. Paul Lewis, *40 Ways to Teach Your Child Values* (Wheaton, IL: Tyndale House Publishers, 1986), p. 123.

3. Ibid., p. 141.

Chapter 24

1. Charles R. Swindoll, *Hand Me Another Brick* (New York: Thomas Nelson, Inc., 1978), p. 36.

2. John C. Maxwell, What Parents Owe Their Children, Psalm 128:1-4, Tape of 93, May 02-1.

3. Merton Strommen, *Five Cries of Youth* (Harper and Row), information from *Moody Monthly*, 1975, Moody Bible Institute of Chicago.

4. Dr. James Dobson, Christian Fathering, Focus on the Family Film Study Guide, Educational Products Division, Word, Inc. Waco, Texas, 1979. p. 7.

5. *Webster's Encyclopedia Unabridged Dictionary* (New York, Avenel, New Jersey, 1989), p. 1502.